"I'll admit it—I couldn't put Anita Agers-Brooks's new book down. If you have ever wondered, *Why am I here?* or perhaps, *Will my life ever get better?*, then you have come to the right place. Anita has a unique and powerful way of weaving stories together with biblical principles that leaves an imprint on your heart that just won't go away. *Exceedingly* will convince you—once and for all—that you were made to live a life of rare and valuable purpose."

—CAROL BURTON McLEOD, radio host, speaker, and best-selling author of *Guide Your Mind, Guard Your Heart, Grace Your Tongue*

"An excellent read from a terrific writer whose faith and wisdom were honed through incredible experiences. As I read this awesome book, I felt extraordinarily moved. Papa God used Anita Agers-Brooks's beautifully descriptive words to wash over me like a cool waterfall on a hot summer day. His still, small voice became remarkably clear: we each have a purpose, a customized reason for our existence, and it's up to us to discern what it is and live it out abundantly. This marvelous book is a great way to start. We feel the raw emotion in Anita's personal stories and eagerly accept the to-do challenges for personal growth at the end of each chapter. The resonance and depth of spot-on discussion questions make *Exceedingly* a great choice for both individuals and groups."

—DEBORA M. COTY, award-winning and best-selling author of the Too Blessed to Be Stressed series

"Anita's phenomenal voice is loaded with intelligence, energy, and authentic feeling. Every story moves the reader to view what is in an entirely different light and state of mind than our everyday tendencies. Opportunity exists—if we are able to see it. When I wrapped up this book, I was in wonder of her ability to invite us into her reality so that we feel like we are right there with her, and so that we can finally understand the rich interconnections between psyche, body, and soul."

—DEB CROWE, Habit Finder life coach and speaker

"From time to time, I pick up a book that encourages, instructs, and inspires my walk with Jesus. *Exceedingly* is definitely one of them. Anita helps us find practical and insightful truth-based promises to live the life we were called to live. Your fears, failures, and frustrations are about to be taken to task with faith, forgiveness, and simple trust in God. Do not read this book if you don't want to be better and live with purpose."

—REV. JEFF ANDERSON, church relations executive director for Convoy of Hope

"Anita Agers-Brooks loves to encourage others to discover their purpose in life. In *Exceedingly*, she shares her exciting and often difficult journey of pursuing her God-given calling. If you need motivation to discern God's plan for your life, you will be inspired by Anita's candid and intriguing stories. Not only will you enjoy her engaging style of storytelling, you will also be captivated by her vulnerability and courageous faith. A great gift for someone trying to find their own purpose and a valuable resource for your personal or group study."

—KAREN JORDAN, author of *Words That Change Everything*

"Anita has the gift of relating to others as if she's known them forever. Through that connection, she helps reveal the person's true passions *and* the obstacles they've been hiding behind. I felt a deep comfort with Anita that caught me by surprise, in the best way. Through a rarely perfected balance of faith-based and empirical coaching, she helped guide me to a renewed sense of purpose and commitment to intentional living."

—PAIGE HULSEY, KMOV-TV anchor and reporter

"Amazing stories of overcoming adversity that produce faith are the central focus of *Exceedingly*. Anita has crafted her book with purpose to motivate you as well as challenge you toward greatness. Practical in every sense, especially the prompting questions at the end of each chapter, this book equips you to find that exceedingly abundant life no matter what you've faced."

—EDDIE JONES, lead pastor of Christian Life Center

"If you only read one book this year, read *Exceedingly.* It is the culmination of years of prayer, work, study, and perseverance. I am personally inspired by Anita's words every time we talk, and now many more people can experience her gift of encouragement."

—KATHRYN GRAVES, author of *Fashioned by God*

"Anita Agers-Brooks is easily one of the most effective and communicative authors I've ever had the privilege of reading. I especially benefited from her uncanny ability to draw the reader into her personal life and story. In fact, she has helped me correctly address some of my own rearview-mirror 'ghosts' that needed the truth of God's Word to be fully set free . . . and to live life exceedingly abundantly and on purpose. This great book has truly blessed my life."

—DALE BROWN, serial entrepreneur and
outdoor adventure crew specialist

"Anita Agers-Brooks has done it again! I found myself enthralled by the stories in this book. She has created not just a cover-to-cover read but a manual for life that includes a culmination of story and Scripture. Relatable and on point as always, this is a resource you can pick up to find wisdom for whatever season you may be walking through."

—ASHLEY CAUDLE, human resources administrator

also by ANITA AGERS-BROOKS

First Hired, Last Fired

Getting Through What You Can't Get Over

CODE: Living Healthy, Happy, and Whole Submerged in Tragedy, Trauma, and Death (with Darren Dake)

Death Defied, Life Defined (with Paul E. Perkins)

Now to Him who is able to do **EXCEEDINGLY** *abundantly above all that we ask or think, according to the power that works in us.*

SPIRITUAL STRATEGIES FOR LIVING
ON PURPOSE, WITH PURPOSE,
AND FOR AN ABUNDANT PURPOSE

ANITA AGERS-BROOKS

Kregel
Publications

Exceedingly: Spiritual Strategies for Living on Purpose, with Purpose, and for an Abundant Purpose

Published by Kregel Publications, a division of Kregel Inc., 2450 Oak Industrial Dr. NE, Grand Rapids, MI 49505.

The persons and events portrayed in this book have been used with permission. Some names and identifying details have been changed.

Published in association with the literary agency of WordServe Literary Group, Ltd., www.wordserveliterary.com.

Cover verse (Ephesians 3:20) taken from the New King James Version.

ISBN 978-0-8254-4564-4, print
ISBN 978-0-8254-7549-8, epub

Printed in the United States of America
19 20 21 22 23 24 25 26 27 28 / 5 4 3 2 1

To my mom,
the woman who gave birth to me and so much more.

She taught me to live my life with dignity and respect for others, and above all else, to put God first.

My whole existence, I've watched my mother strive to live out the words she instilled in her children. Though it has often been invisible to her, I can see God's magnificent purpose manifested in all her days.

She has made a difference, left an imprint, and made the world a better place—all because she influenced those placed across her path. I am who I am because my mother is who she is.

I am grateful.

CONTENTS

FOREWORD

The word *abundance* has been tossed around in Christian churches for decades. Often it is used without context, making people believe that an abundant life is merely a pain-free and problem-free joyride. But that's a myth. No such life exists. A person presenting that kind of abundant life needs a reality check.

As I've studied abundant life biblically, I've become convinced that it is lived boldly with passion and purpose for the glory of God. Here's the thing—if I were going to read a book about that kind of life, I would want to be sure the person who wrote the book has actually experienced a few problems. But I would also want to know that, despite those trials, she has learned the secret of living victoriously with purpose. I would want to be sure the author authentically embraced boldness and that she wasn't just presenting an unrealistic plan for a safe, problem-free life.

That's exactly why I am so happy to write the foreword for Anita's book. If anyone has lived life boldly for the glory of God, it's Anita! Her life has been anything but pain free and problem free. She has experienced trials most of us would never want to face. Yet she lives with joyful passion and exuberant purpose. She has found the secret to resiliency, and her bold faith and intentioned gratitude are contagious. Whenever I'm with Anita, I'm inspired. I walk away refreshed and reignited to live an abundant life. That's why I'm thrilled you've picked up this book.

The truth is that Jesus wants you to live an abundant life. In John 10:10, he stated emphatically that he had come for that very reason. He knew you needed an intervention, and not just any intervention, mind you! What Jesus offers will radically transform your life and give you abundant purpose.

If you feel like you're stuck or that you aren't quite living the life you were meant to live, allow Anita to help you find your way. Brilliantly and beautifully, Anita unpacks what a life of passionate purpose looks like. Filled with biblical truth and stories to illustrate, this book is a treat!

Before you dive in, I want to challenge you. Take a few moments to consider where you're at: Are you fulfilled? Are you living boldly and passionately, or is fear holding you back? Do you feel stuck in unforgiveness or bitterness? Is anxiety keeping you up at night? Are you living the dreams that God has placed in your heart, or are there still untended dreams lying in the soil of your soul? Have you taken any risks lately, or do you prefer to keep life safe and predictable? What desire has God placed in your heart that is still unfulfilled?

After you've considered those questions, spend a few moments praying and asking the Holy Spirit to use this book in your life in extraordinary ways. Ask him to open your heart to what he wants to teach you. Then bow and humbly commit to receive all he has for you. In fact, I highly recommend that you journey through this book with a friend or a group of friends! That way you'll have accountability as you consider your unique purpose.

As I write this, I'm praying for you; I'm convinced that he has exceedingly more than all you can think or imagine because he loves you so very much! Have fun as you read. Your abundant adventure awaits.

—BECKY HARLING, host of the *Beyond Beautiful* podcast; certified John Maxwell coach; and author of *How to Listen So People Will Talk*, *Who Do You Say That I Am?*, and other titles

INTRODUCTION

When asked, few people I meet in my travels as a speaker and author, or while I am at home with friends or family, tell me they live an abundant life. Though I understand this from an experiential level, it saddens me. We were made for abundance. How do I know? Because God clearly tells us so.

Ephesians 3:20 promises, "Now to Him who is able to do exceedingly abundantly above all that we ask or think, according to the power that works in us . . ." (NKJV). Read this verse again—carefully. How many of us are plugging in to this Source and receiving the benefits of his power?

The Bible is clear: we were made to live life more—exceedingly abundantly more. John 10:10 says, "The thief does not come except to steal, and to kill, and to destroy. I have come that they may have life, and that they may have it more abundantly" (NKJV). So let me ask you: Are you living in abundance?

If not, I hope that by the time you finish reading this book, you will already see a transformation taking place. I believe God wants you to know that you were made on purpose, with a purpose, and for a purpose. Sometimes God gently introduces us to our purposes. More often, he uses drastic measures.

And I am no different. My journey to living exceedingly started in 1997.

My youngest sister needed an organ transplant, and for me, there was no hesitation or question. I would test and see if I matched. I did.

On Monday, May 19, 1997, doctors opened up my left side and removed my kidney, then immediately placed it inside my sister's body. The surgery went well for both of us. But by Wednesday, my condition spiraled.

Throughout the transplant testing process, doctors, nurses, and other specialists asked me the same question over and over. I heard it so much, I got tired of answering. But I dutifully played along.

Each medical professional said, "Are you allergic to any medications?"

I answered, "Not that I'm aware of."

"Good." Chart noted.

But in the days following my surgery, I discovered I was allergic to something—Dilaudid.

By the wee hours of Friday morning, my blood pressure was about 64/36, and my oxygen was 70. I could feel my body shutting down as my life on earth slipped away. In desperation, I began to pray.

It was only in those terrifying moments when I couldn't breathe that God finally got my full attention. He'd pursued me for quite some time, but I had repeatedly tuned him out and turned down his invitations. I had been too busy to slow down and listen to God. Truthfully, I often wondered if he even existed.

But in my near death, my true beginning was birthed. There's nothing like getting kicked in the gut with the reality of life's short span to help you realize the importance of seeking your purpose and fulfilling it while you still can. The running stopped, and as I allowed myself to hear the urgency of God's whispers, I began to understand what he wanted for my life.

Back then, I felt utterly ordinary, untalented, and inadequate. But God kept sending one prevailing message. Through books, interviews, movies, everyday conversations, and the Bible, his voice rang in my thoughts: "I made you for more than mere existence. I handcrafted and designed you with a special plan in mind. You have a purpose."

The challenge for me, and for all of us, was figuring out what that amazing purpose was, something I now call my "high calling." What did abundant living look like, and how could I have it?

I was just beginning to understand what Jesus meant when he promised us life to the full on the day I met a celebrity—though I didn't know who he was at first. This manuscript is a result of our meeting.

In a single day, Troy became my friend. I am sad to say he died very recently, at a young age, just before I was able to share the news that

Kregel Publications had bought this book. My friend would have been happy, maybe even ecstatic, since the news might have helped answer the question he asked the day we met. The question many others have asked me since.

Because of who he was, Troy's heartfelt query speaks to the burning desire every man and woman wrestles with. No matter who we are, we all have inquiring minds; we need to know why we're alive.

Missouri Augusts are typically hot and humid, especially around noon. Thursday, August 23, 2012, was typical. Sweat rolled down the center of my back while I brainstormed with radio execs about sound-check schedules, green-room meals, and backstage access for VIP fans. At the time, I was the general manager of Ozark Outdoors Riverfront Resort, and we were discussing our tenth annual music festival, partnering with one of St. Louis's biggest country radio stations.

I'll be up front right now: the entertainment industry is not typically a Christian climate. But I've watched God's hand at work in it more times than I can count. Like Jesus turning water into wine at a wedding reception, God will unveil a plan at times and places you never expect.

That day, eight of us stood in a circle talking details. A dark-haired man approached. I didn't see him at first. But I looked up when I heard his deep, warm, male voice. He offered me his hand. "Hi. I'm Troy."

His clothes were ordinary fare for a country-music stagehand or lighting tech—jeans and a tee shirt. I thought he was one of those guys, since dozens of them milled around.

I simply smiled, shook his hand, and said, "Hi. I'm Anita. Nice to meet you."

He tilted his head slightly as we released. "You don't know who I am, do you?"

I instantly said, "No. Should I?"

Have you ever had that moment when the words slipped from your lips before you even knew they were coming? That's exactly what happened. I felt bad immediately. I hadn't meant to sound rude. But I was so absorbed in the necessities of what we needed to accomplish that I spoke mindlessly.

The man gave me a half grin, one of those sly "I know something you don't know" looks. He did a slow-motion, 180-degree turn backward. The speed of his words was as measured as his rotation. "I'm. Troy. Gentry. Of Montgomery Gentry." He pointed to one of the super-luxury artist's buses parked neatly behind us. Then he grinned slower and wider. "That's my picture. Right there." His statement wasn't boastful, merely playful.

I didn't want to offend, but I'm also not one to fawn over celebrities. I'd met quite a few famous, wealthy, and powerful people through some pretty unusual situations and found all of them to be as human as the rest of us. This is why it wasn't out of character for me to carry on—as if he hadn't just come off a whirlwind concert tour, including stops at major New York morning television shows. I was simply being myself when I responded to his picture pointing.

I tried to maintain my professional composure. "I apologize that I didn't recognize you. I'm the manager here at Ozark Outdoors, but I actually don't listen to much country music. Sorry."

He chuckled from his belly, as if he was pleasantly amused. "That's okay. But do you mind my asking what you do listen to? If you listen to music at all."

I quickly warmed to his easygoing manner. "I don't mind a bit. I mostly listen to contemporary Christian. My faith is very important to me."

His face lit up. "I love contemporary Christian music. That's so cool."

"I think so."

We chitchatted a bit, small talk mostly. Then he asked me where he could find the closest workout place.

I laughed out loud at that one. "You aren't in the city. The closest workout you're going to get is jogging down the gravel road outside of our entrance. The nearest gym is thirty minutes away."

"Perfect. Thanks, Anita."

"My pleasure," I said, turning back to the business at hand. However, my conversation with Troy did not end there.

About two and a half hours later, I made a stop at the green-room area to make sure things were in order for the artists and working crews who needed to eat and relax before the music festival started. I saw Troy's duo partner, Eddie Montgomery, their bandmates, and the rest of their entourage at a table. Not wanting to disrupt, I simply smiled, nodded, and walked on.

But as I came out of the kitchen, I stopped when I saw Troy walk in the door.

"Got my workout," he said with a smile. Looking rather proud of himself, he sat down to join Eddie and their crew.

I chuckled, then went to work checking in with our resort staff. When I came out of the kitchen a second time, Troy, Eddie, and the rest of their group were standing up to leave. But Troy surprised me. By the expressions on their faces, he apparently astonished his crew too.

He looked straight at me and said, "You guys go on ahead. I'd like to talk to this lady."

I stopped, curious more than anything.

A big guy, who I can only assume must have been part of their security detail, said, "I'll wait with you."

"No. That's okay. You go on ahead. I'd like to talk to her alone."

I confess I didn't know what to think.

Someone else in the group said, "We've got sound checks in an hour."

Troy answered firmly, "I know. Don't worry, I'll be there. I just want to talk to her before we start. All right?"

The group left, and Troy navigated me outside, onto the large, wraparound resort deck for privacy. He didn't waste any time getting to his point. "It was refreshing to hear you talk so openly about your faith today. I don't get to hear a lot of positive talk about God on the road, and your transparency was inspiring. You weren't pushy about it, but you also didn't hide it. It just felt natural."

I admit I was stunned. But the shocks didn't end there.

With a tinge of pink to his cheeks, Troy looked me directly in the eyes and continued. "You can imagine some of the mistakes I've made. Being on the road is tough on a marriage, but my wife is an angel. Actually, her name is Angie, so it fits." He smiled wide.

I noted the tenderness in his tone. It was my turn to feel refreshed, hearing a man honor his wife behind her back.

Troy seemed to be on a mission with what he wanted to say, so he didn't leave much time for my reflections. For several minutes, his face shone as he shared more about his love and admiration for Angie and how much he adored his daughters. But he was also interested in hearing my faith story.

He listened intently when I told him about things I'd been through and how God was using them to reveal his magnificent plan for my life. The more I talked, the more serious Troy became. I noticed the sparkle increase in both of his eyes as they watered.

He leaned just a little closer, as if he wanted to share a conspiratorial secret. I didn't guess what he would say next.

"Anita, do you mind if I ask you a question?"

"Not at all," I said.

"How did you discover your true purpose? How do I find out what God's purpose is for me? I'm not sure I'm living the life God wants."

I pulled back a little, surprised by his questions. Here was a guy who, night after night, stood on a stage while screaming fans shouted his name. I'd seen his tour bus; it was gorgeous. He didn't hurt for money, and from his description, Troy had a beautiful home with a wife he treasured. He explained how homesick he often felt, missing time with his girls. He appeared to be a man who had all the toys a guy could want and plenty of friends to share them with. People clamored to be close to him. He had the fame and fortune most people desire. And yet, these important questions burned in his heart. *Am I doing what God wants me to do with my life? Is this all there is? Am I experiencing everything I'm supposed to?*

We talked at length. I shared my story about how God finally showed me that I was supposed to write.

When I asked if he had a home church, Troy said he did. He told me he attended every chance he could off tour. I encouraged him to speak with his pastor and to search the Bible while asking God to make his purpose clear. "Keep looking until it becomes obvious," I told him.

The last time I saw him was later that night, just before he boarded his bus. Troy suddenly turned back. He walked up to me and asked, "Would you mind if we stayed in touch?"

"If you'd like," I said.

"I would." He grinned. "I could use an extra boost of faith every now and then." He leaned down and wrote his email address on the back of a restaurant ticket.

I jotted mine on the edge of a napkin.

We didn't correspond regularly. Both of us led busy lives. But occasionally, one of us would reach out to the other with a word of encouragement or piece of news. He was especially excited the day he let me know his youngest daughter was getting baptized after asking Jesus Christ to be a part of her life. I was thrilled for him.

On September 8, 2017, Troy tragically died in a helicopter crash. We had just emailed a couple weeks prior—nothing special, just a benign exchange between friends. I never dreamed it would be our last communication on earth. His death hit me hard. But it also spurred me to wonder . . . *Did Troy feel his questions were answered? If not, could writing this book play a role in seeing Troy Gentry's abundant purpose fulfilled?*

I'm not sure, but I'm willing to explore the possibility that this body of work could help unveil the meaning Troy was made for. If through his story one person decides to passionately seek the real reason for their existence, then Troy made a lasting impact beyond what many might have imagined.

Most people looked at Troy through the eyes of celebrity. I saw a friend who was also an emboldened seeker. Not because of me, but for him, I've often wondered if one of the last songs Troy recorded, "Better Me," had anything to do with our exchange. Only God truly knows.

If questions like Troy's ring through your mind, I pray you find answers in this book. If you realize life is short, and you want to experience all that God desires for you while you can, my hope is to provide inspiration as well as practical prompts. At the end of each chapter, I'll share brief but powerful insights, called Mind, Body, and Spirit Strengtheners, to help you discover why you exist and what God desires for you to know about your life. These are designed to help you reach deep within, so you can pull out all you were made to be. God's favor doesn't depend on position or platform; his promises exist for everyday people. *You* were made for an abundant purpose. The question is, do you believe it?

CHAPTER 1

Made for Abundant Purpose

We are what we believe we are.

—Benjamin N. Cardozo

Why on earth are *you* here? Why was *I* made? Why are you breathing? Why am I alive? These are questions most of us ask, often regularly. Who doesn't want to unearth the real reason they exist?

Some people wonder if they're even supposed to take up space on this planet, possibly believing they are an accident or some cosmic mix-up. Does this describe you? Are you afraid to believe you deserve more?

Or perhaps your issue isn't wondering but wandering.

Are you tired of doing nothing but existing—getting up, going through the same old motions, stumbling through life in a zombielike trance? Do you feel like there should be more?

Or do you fall in the camp of those who have gotten a glimpse of something more? You know your purpose but feel stifled in living it out. Are you fired up, much like a Thoroughbred behind the gate, stomping and snorting, waiting to be released? Are you ready for more?

If any of these scenarios describe you, I have great news. Those stirrings in the deepest part of your soul are there for a reason: you *are* made for more. You were made *on* purpose, *with* purpose, and you are meant to *fulfill* an abundant purpose. As a person created in the image of God, your Creator, you are marked for more than a humdrum, stuck-in-a-rut, there-has-to-be-more-than-this life.

As we go through our days, something inside our human spirits whispers to us, "You are marked for more," but discovering precisely what our purpose is can seem as elusive as a cool drink in a hot desert. Often, the more we hunger for an answer, the less satisfied we feel.

Two Essential Questions

If you're like me, I suspect there are two essential questions you have asked at least once, either in the privacy of your own thoughts or verbalized publicly to anyone who might provide a clear answer.

Why was I born?

What happens when we die?

The earliest memory I have of these questions comes from when I was a child.

I remember the rising summer sun streaming through my bedroom window. I turned my head beneath the covers in hopes of returning to my former dreamy state. Our house was so still that my stomach's growl sounded ten times louder than normal. At first I wanted sleep more than food, but then my belly won out.

No one else was awake as I walked to the kitchen and reached far above my head to pull a fresh tomato off the counter. Thanks to Mom's gardening skills, we always had organically grown vegetables and fruits in season.

As I bit into the soft, crimson flesh, tomato juice and seeds gushed out of my mouth. The acidic flavor burst across my tongue, and strange thoughts sparked inside my young brain.

Where did the first tomato come from? Who created tomatoes? Why were they made? How did a big red tomato come out of the tiny white seeds we planted in the ground?

And then, for some unknown reason, a deeper question followed. *Why was I born?*

Why these musings came at such a tender age, I don't know, but I suddenly felt an odd compulsion to know the answer. Even stranger, I simultaneously had a soul-deep inner knowledge of an important truth: I was made for something special. These stirrings have never left me.

At that time, I somehow felt absolutely confident. Someone had made me on purpose. Later in my life, I would come to question that fact, especially when other voices had a chance to rewire my thinking and new information about myself surfaced. But even then, after much investigation and soul-searching (I'll share details of that quest as we go), I would once again arrive at the same conclusion.

I exist for a reason. A unique, extraordinary, and powerful intention was grafted in me when I was formed in my mother's womb.

I was made for more. The same is true for you.

A second, mysterious question came to me within days of the first while I was playing outside. This memory is as vivid as the first.

Next to the house I grew up in stood a massive cedar tree. Pieces of its ancient bark curled off of the trunk, releasing a strong evergreen aroma. Sometimes I would sit beneath the blanket of its dense branches, hiding from the world, nestled in the soft yet prickly bed of loose needles covering the ground. Other times, the happy tomboy in me would scale the thick branch hovering mere inches above the needle-carpeted soil. From there, it was easy to traverse from limb to limb, making my way higher than my mom would have allowed—if she knew.

It never took me long to arrive at my favorite spot: a hammock-shaped merge of two strong branches near the top. It was the perfect crook for me to burrow into while the wind swung and swayed, making the cedar trunk creak and the needles murmur. Maybe the distance from my perch to the ground is what caused the second question to flit across my young brain.

What happens when we die?

As an adult, I know I'm not alone in my musings. From speaking to many women and men through the years, I've found that most people want answers to the same two questions.

1. Why do we exist?
2. What happens when we die?

I shared my story about finding answers to the second question in my book *Getting Through What You Can't Get Over*, so I won't readdress the topic here. Instead, for *Exceedingly*, I want to explore and share my experiences, and those of others, in solving the mystery of the first matter. *Why* do *we exist?*

An Answer

Not so long ago, my own quest for discovering why I exist came roaring back to the forefront, through the revelation of an almost fifty-year-old secret.

The year was 2010. I was forty-six. Not the age you expect to discover a life-changing disclosure about yourself.

When I awoke on the morning of September 23, I felt good as I settled into a chair on my back deck, unaware that stunning news was on the way.

Warm sunlight dappled the fading green oak leaves surrounding my outdoor haven. A couple of cheerful warblers tweeted background music while I worked. A silken breeze brushed my cheeks and shuffled my notebook pages, forcing me to stop typing on my computer. I put things back in place and took a sip of bubbling ginger ale before placing my fingers on the keyboard again. I was searching for the perfect verb to strengthen my sentence when a ping interrupted my thoughts—the ping that started a cascade of events that challenged everything I believed about myself.

The Facebook notification alerted me to a private message from an acquaintance of over thirty years. My friend asked a question about her attempts to find the identity of her biological father, hoping I might offer direction or advice. We ended up meeting for dinner, and I took copious notes, particularly when we discussed the possibility of DNA testing with someone I knew who was a potential candidate. We would eventually find out he was not her biological dad. But her search set me on my own quest—one I didn't see coming.

A few days later, on the phone with my mom, I asked what I believed was a rhetorical question. To this day, I'm not sure why those specific words crossed my mind, compelling me to voice them out loud. The only explanation I have is God's prompting. I was chuckling while they spilled from my lips. I was sure I knew the answer—yet, I asked anyway.

"Mom. Dad is absolutely my father. Right?"

Her reaction was unexpected and instantaneous.

Guttural sobs stilted her sentences. "I'm. So. Sorry. I never. Wanted to hurt you." She sucked air and moaned. "I knew I'd have to tell you someday. I didn't want to cause you any pain."

My laughter turned to shock. I couldn't believe what I was hearing. What was my mom telling me?

I crumpled onto my bed. A rippling heat started inside my skull, spreading down my face, neck, arms, chest, torso, legs, all the way into my toes. I heard myself speaking, though my brain seemed disconnected from my mouth.

"What? What are you saying? Are you telling me that Dad isn't my father?"

Mom sniffled. "No. I'm not saying that—I think he is."

And there it was. A secret my mom had kept for almost fifty years—a secret about me.

Mom finally calmed enough to tell me the story of a young man she had worked with in 1963 at a burger joint called the Hi-Spot, in Corona, California. He lived in an apartment behind her house and invited her in on Halloween. It was just three months before her eighteenth birthday. She went to show him the cowboy shirt and hat she wore for the occasion. But when she entered his apartment, the click of the lock behind her changed everything.

Two days later, my mom met my dad at my uncle's wedding rehearsal. The following evening, after the nuptials, Mom and Dad enjoyed the reception, along with some adult refreshments.

As my mother told the story, I could hear the poignancy in her voice.

Especially when she said, "I remember the moment clearly. I thought, *What am I saving myself for anyway? At least this time it will be my choice.*"

And so three days apart, two potential conceptions occurred.

As Mom finished, I felt light-headed and breathless. Her unexpected revelation raised a new question inside my brain, demanding an answer.

Who is my father?

We got off the phone shortly after Mom finished telling me her secret. I felt dazed.

I was blindsided about the questionable nature of my identity and, wondering what the future might hold, I was a mess. My poor husband watched helplessly, afraid to say much of anything—but he did the best thing possible: he held me while I cried.

I slept little and got up early the next morning. Wanting to occupy my mind, I drove to work, hoping productivity would distract me. But the prevailing question of who I was plagued me. If my dad wasn't my dad, what did that mean for me? Was I still a loved, desired child or merely a by-product of another man's sins?

Within weeks, DNA results provided the truth of my biology. I was an emotional wreck by the time the emailed report hit my inbox. I expected a particular result. Instead, the truth pulled the rug from beneath my world—it said my dad was *not* my biological father.

Suddenly, everything I thought I knew about myself was wiped away. Now I had to come to terms with not only who I was but how I was conceived.

Instantly, I went from feeling like a grown, mature woman to feeling like that child all those years before who had asked, *Why was I born?*

My nervous system was on full overload. No other human being knew what I was wrestling with deep inside the darkness of my soul.

I cried for three solid nights and days, hardly eating, barely drinking, getting little sleep. By the end of that period, my eyes were almost swollen shut. Alone in my house that third afternoon, sitting on my couch, I closed my eyes and imagined myself in the body of the little girl who now controlled my mind. A little girl who needed her daddy. And I made a decision.

Mentally, I scurried up into my Daddy God's lap. I laid my head against his chest and wailed, releasing my confusion and pain into his care. Telling him all the things I'd bottled up over the previous days, I expressed my fear of being an accident—someone he probably regretted allowing to exist. The ugliness I felt over how I was created poured out.

Then it happened.

I felt a sensation, as if my heavenly Father brushed my bangs across my forehead, away from my eyes. He stroked my cheek. He kissed the tip of my nose, tilted my chin up, and kissed it too. Then he whispered in my ear, "Daddy's here. You are not alone. You are wanted. I love you. You look like me."

I lay there for a very long time, hiccupping like a young child at the end of a hard cry.

Finally, when I felt somewhat composed, I prayed.

> *Daddy God,*
>
> *You know all of the things hurting my heart right now. You especially know how I feel about myself, the things I've told no one else. Could you please do something for me? I'm going to open my Bible, trusting you to speak to me from it, and could you give me something really personal? Could you make it so plain that I know it's a private word from you?*

I opened my burning eyes and picked up the NIV Bible next to me. Then I closed my eyes again and gently tugged on each side of the cover.

The tissue-like pages fluttered softly, whispering as they fell on top of each other. When the sounds stopped, I opened my eyes again, and I saw chapter fifteen in the book of John. I was familiar with the passage, but the precise verse my eyes were drawn to did not stir any memory. It was as if I'd never seen it before, though by now I'd read through the Bible multiple times.

I read John 15:3 silently at first—then again out loud. "You are already clean because of the word I have spoken to you."

For the first time since I'd opened the DNA test results, I smiled. The message penetrated my empty living room and infused my aching spirit. Only God had known just how much the facts of my conception hurt both me and my mother. Only my heavenly Father knew how worthless and impure I felt. Only he knew the depth of compassion I carried for my mom, the seventeen-year-old who chose to allow me life. My mom needed my understanding, not condemnation—she'd carried undeserved guilt far too long already.

That day, alone on my couch, I received from God exactly what I requested, a personal word, both special and plain, yet powerful in its cathartic touch. It was the beginning of a long healing journey, one that would ultimately prove to me why I was born. But God had a lot more to teach me first.

When I share this story from a speaking platform, people ask me afterward if I've tried to find my biological father. The answer is yes, but not like I did immediately following my discovery. I haven't given up on finding him entirely, but where I searched obsessively the first couple of years, today I've stopped allowing the hunt to control my life. I've asked God to protect me if it would be unhealthy or even dangerous for me to find my biological father, but to also provide a miracle if it is safe. My trust is in the Lord.

Learning the truth of my identity caused me much grief at first, but it also taught me to crawl into my Daddy God's lap. It was there that the Father to the fatherless told me who I really am (Ps. 68:5).

I now know I am not defined by my conception and DNA. I exist on purpose, with purpose, and for a purpose no other human being can fulfill.

But my story isn't just about me—it's also about you.

God's Plan for You

I don't know the story of your conception, but I do know this: before birth, you were designed, planned, and created in intricate detail (Ps. 139:13–14). You were marked uniquely for greatness—though its expression may be seen by one, by many, or by you and your heavenly Father alone.

Science still cannot figure out many of the miraculous ways our human bodies operate. I believe this single piece of evidence points to our Maker's existence. The grand Creator made you because he desires a relationship with you (Acts 17:26–27).

We were made to be loved. We were marked for more. *You* were made on purpose, with purpose, for an abundant purpose.

But most of us miss these important truths. Even in God's greatest commands, we often overlook one of the most important foundational pieces.

I pray that by the time you finish this book, you will be transformed as God awes you through the treasure of the purity of his plan for you. You were not made to simply exist; you exist for exceedingly more.

MIND, BODY, AND SPIRIT STRENGTHENERS

YOUR ABUNDANT PURPOSE CHALLENGE

Look at yourself in the mirror with fresh eyes. You are made in the image of God. You! What new things do you see about yourself?

YOUR ABUNDANT PURPOSE EXERCISE

Daily, for the next month, express gratitude for at least one thing about your life. Write each down in a notebook. Then review all of them at the end of thirty days.

YOUR ABUNDANT PURPOSE SCRIPTURE

Psalm 139:13–14: "You made all the delicate, inner parts of my body and knit me together in my mother's womb. Thank you for making me so wonderfully complex! Your workmanship is marvelous—how well I know it."

YOUR ABUNDANT PURPOSE PROMISE

You exist on purpose, with purpose, for a purpose.

YOUR ABUNDANT PURPOSE STUDY AND DISCUSSION PROMPTS

Are you comfortable in your own skin?

Is your conception and childhood story "normal"? Why or why not?

Do you see God as a loving Daddy who will allow you to scurry up into his lap so he can love on you?

CHAPTER 2

Made for Love

When you love much, you are forgiven much—
and when you are forgiven much, you love much.

—Søren Kierkegaard, *Discourses at the Communion on Fridays*

Have you ever looked at someone else and thought, *I wish I had her life? She's got it made. It seems like someone waved a magic wand over her. When I compare myself to her, I realize I don't need a makeover, I need a whole life do-over.*

How is it that we appreciate the gifts others receive but often overlook our own? We view certain people and think, *I can understand why God would bless him but not me. I'm not as good as that person. I don't have her talents and abilities. I'm a mess. I just don't have anything to offer the world like he does.*

Why is it easier for many of us to hate the person we see in the mirror rather than love that person? I mean a healthy, balanced, humble kind of love—the sort of love defined by seeing ourselves through God's eyes.

Most of us are guilty of trying to change at least one other person into someone very different from who they were created to be—ourselves. From a young age, many of us attempt to make over who we are, afraid that our original design isn't good enough. We're scared that we've made too many mistakes, so we try to cover up our sins with masks.

By the time we are adults, we've become so adept at our efforts, we don't realize or recognize how second nature these habits are or how far we've distanced ourselves from the spirit of our original design.

Several years ago, the dangerous consequences of this sad pattern jumped out at me as I read what many refer to as the greatest biblical command. In Mark 12:28, a religious teacher asks Jesus which of God's commands is most important.

Verses 29–31 record Christ's answer: "The most important commandment is this: 'Listen, O Israel! The LORD our God is the one and only LORD. And you must love the LORD your God with all your heart, all your soul, all your mind, and all your strength.' The second is equally important: 'Love your neighbor as yourself.' No other commandment is greater than these."

Though I'd read this passage numerous times, something new caught my eye. How had I overlooked it?

I suddenly saw the part telling me to love my neighbor as myself. The thought made me feel a bit squeamish.

As myself? Looking in the rearview mirror of my life, loving myself didn't carry much appeal.

However, I realized I couldn't love my neighbor if I didn't love me.

An epiphany struck me—I had stopped loving the woman in the mirror when I started hating her for her failures. This was especially true in 2001, when life for me felt very dark.

After my near death in 1997, I experienced debilitating anxiety attacks and depression. I was finally beginning to feel somewhat normal again when I was forced to face my greatest fear.

In 1999, I found out my husband had had an affair. By July 23, 2001, we were both working hard to save our marriage. But that day I committed my own massive betrayal.

A Heartbreaking Lesson

We were visiting my family in New Mexico, scattered in and around Albuquerque. The temperature was over one hundred on that mid-July Monday. The dry high-desert heat radiated off the black asphalt, warping the horizon we were driving toward in vertical waves.

For my birthday that year, Mom suggested we visit Sky City, home of the Acoma Native American tribe. I've always had a fascination with those who live off the land, whether it's the Amish, the Ingalls family, or ancient people groups like the Acoma, who live high on a sheer-walled, 367-foot New Mexican sandstone bluff called a mesa. Continuously inhabited for two thousand years, the Acoma Pueblo is one of the oldest continuous communities in the United States.

As my husband, mother, and I traveled west on I-40, centered in the brown expanse of nothing but sand, cactus, and tumbleweed, we suddenly came upon two convenience stores in the middle of nowhere. Bowlin's Trading Post sat on our westbound lane, and Laguna Travel Center waited across the highway for travelers moving east.

Our parched mouths watered at the thought of cool drinks.

Prior to my I-40 experience, I'd prayed, asking God to speak clearly to me so I would know it was him and not just my own mind playing tricks on me.

My friend Darla had recently given me a good rule of thumb to follow: pay attention when you get the same or a very similar message from three different places or people. And of course, she cautioned me to read the Bible for myself, so I would become familiar with God's character and voice. I was on my second time reading through the Bible, cover to cover.

Have you ever been told to be careful what you pray for?

As soon as I got inside the convenience store, a voice spoke clearly inside my head—and it certainly wasn't mine because I would never tell myself what I was being directed to do.

See the woman behind the counter? I want you to go pray with her.

My husband and mom had both walked in different directions to other areas of the store, so I was alone. My steps stuttered, but I kept walking, my face turned toward the checkout counter as I moved. Behind the cash register, the dark-haired, middle-aged woman with a pleasant face lit up with a pretty smile, acknowledging my presence.

I smiled back sheepishly, thankful she couldn't read my mind.

I answered the voice in my head mentally but desperately. *I can't do that. I don't know that woman. She'll think I'm crazy.*

I confess to feeling a little miffed that the first time God would speak to me in such a clear way, he would ask something like this of me.

He was adamant. *Do it anyway. Pray with her.*

She will think I'm nuts. She's never met me before in her life.

Pray with her.

I don't know how long I stood there mentally debating with God, but eventually, with trembling fingers, I selected a drink and slowly walked toward the counter. My heart felt like a conga drum, keeping a quadruple-time rhythm in harmony with my steps. My cheeks, ears, and neck burned and throbbed. I tried to swallow, but my mouth felt like the dry expanse outside.

As I approached the counter hesitantly, the woman's head was down while she wrote on a piece of paper. But then something caught my eye, and I stopped, six to eight paces from the stranger God wanted me to pray with.

Her name tag read Linda. And that's all it took. That was the name of the woman my husband had had the affair with.

You know I cannot pray with her, I told God. *I'll pray for her—silently.*

She looked up. "Can I help you find something?"

I looked down and mumbled. "No thanks. I just need to check out."

"No problem." I caught a glimpse of her sweet smile one more time as she patiently waited for me to hand her my drink.

While she scanned my soda, I threw a quick prayer toward heaven, while I avoided her eyes.

Lord, I don't know why you want me to pray with this lady, but please forgive me. I can't do it, especially since she has the same name as that woman. Whatever is going on with her, please take care of her. In Jesus's name. Amen.

Then I hurried out of the store, stuffing my emotions, justifying my concession. For some reason, I felt compelled to look at my watch. It was 4:07 p.m.

Neither my husband nor my mom had any idea about what had occurred, as they joked together, getting back into the car. A few miles down the road, Mom said to me, "Are you okay? You're awfully quiet."

"I'm fine. Just thinking about Sky City," I lied.

It took a while for my heart to finally settle into a normalized beat, as I replayed the scenario over and over. Ultimately, I convinced myself that I'd been at least somewhat obedient, by praying *for* the Linda behind the register, even though I hadn't followed God's instructions precisely. I had no idea the story wasn't over. In less than two hours' time, I'd be forced to face my decision again.

We arrived at Sky City around 4:50 and were disappointed when the cashier told us ticket sales had closed. We'd just missed the cutoff for the last trip up the Acoma Pueblo.

We had no choice but to turn around and take Highway 40 eastbound, back toward Albuquerque.

While we were driving, we saw a local tourist attraction and pulled in to look around. I'd finally put my earlier conviction to bed mentally—covering it with a blanket of distraction.

Soon, we were back on the road, chatting, laughing, enjoying the day. Until . . .

Several miles down Highway 40, the car popped over a small rise, and my breath caught in my throat. I looked at the clock in our vehicle. It was 6:01 p.m.

One hundred fourteen minutes after I'd checked my watch upon leaving Bowlin's Trading Post, emergency vehicles were everywhere—on both sides of the interstate. New Mexico State Highway Patrol cars flashed red and blue, sitting amid a tangle of ambulances and sheriff's cars. A big fire truck sat near where we had pulled in, such a short time before, only at a catty-corner angle.

Then I noticed the sound coming from the sky, a deep thrumming, that seemed to reverberate into our vehicle. I looked up, where the thump of helicopter blades circled just south of us. My gut scrunched, like I'd just eaten a bad meal. I didn't know exactly what had occurred at Bowlin's Trading Post, but I couldn't deny—it was bad.

Once we passed the throng of emergency vehicles, all I could think about was finding out what had happened, though I dreaded the answer. One of my sisters lived on the west side of Albuquerque. I urged my husband, "Can you go faster? I need to know what happened. Drive to Deanne's house, she's closest to where we are."

He didn't question me, but pushed the gas pedal harder as we drove toward my sister's place.

My husband barely had the car parked before I jumped out in my sister's driveway. I ran into the house, ignoring pleasantries and turned on her TV.

We huddled in front of the screen, where "Breaking News" flashed across the bottom of the emerging picture. A reporter's voice narrated the action at the scene. A manhunt for three men was underway. They had committed multiple murders, including one at Bowlin's Trading Post. The victims' names would not be disclosed until family members were notified, but I knew in my heart, one was Linda. Now I understood why God's directive to pray *with* her was so important.

I got up and ran to the bathroom—so I wouldn't vomit in front of my family.

The next morning's edition of the *Albuquerque Journal* confirmed what I suspected. The woman murdered at Bowlin's Trading Post was the woman I'd refused to pray with—her name was Linda Chavez. I still have that yellowed newspaper.

For weeks, I read everything I could find about the case online. I learned that Linda Ann Chavez, a lifelong resident of New Mexico, was fifty-four years old when she was brutally gunned down. She left a husband, two daughters, a stepson, grandchildren, her mother, sisters, and brothers behind. I anguished over how her family must feel.

I also read the account of another employee, hidden in the back, who witnessed Linda's pleas for her life. Chavez begged the murderers to spare her, for her family's sake.

Forgiving Myself

For the longest time, I wrestled with my failure to comply with God's request that day. I can't say exactly what he wanted Linda to know through the prayer he asked me to speak out loud, but I suspect it would have provided assurance, in her final moments, that he saw her and loved what he saw. I believe God wanted her to know he was with her to the very end. Our Father had chosen me to offer her comfort, and I disobeyed.

To this day, I carry the hope that someone came behind me, someone who didn't allow anxiety to stop him or her from fulfilling a purpose far greater than fear—far greater than self.

For a very long time, I couldn't forgive myself for failing Linda Chavez and God, and I told God I didn't blame him for not forgiving me either. I fretted, even wondering if my disobedience jeopardized my entry to heaven. That is, until I realized that if I repent of something I've done wrong—I turn away from committing that type of behavior again—but still refuse to forgive myself, I'm saying I know better than God. If God says I am forgiven, then who am I to say I'm not? This simple realization gave me a fresh outlook.

My refusal to forgive myself had also led to self-hatred—but how could I fulfill God's greatest commandment to love him with my whole heart, soul, mind, and strength, and love my neighbor while detesting myself? Was I hampering God's ability to use me for an extraordinary purpose while I was obsessing over my inadequacy?

I began to search my soul, asking myself a series of questions.

If I despised myself, wasn't I despising God's creation?

What did detesting someone God calls precious, wonderful, holy, and free say to the Maker of the universe?

And what about my neighbor? How could I show love to another person when I didn't even know how to express love to myself?

What if God wanted me to participate in his greater good, but I was denying his power to use me?

I've learned many people struggle with self-acceptance. Does any of this resonate with you? Have you ever asked the kinds of questions I asked? Is guilt, fear, pessimism, insecurity, anxiety, comparison thinking, or just plain, old-fashioned self-loathing preventing you from playing a role in the Master's plan?

If so, take heart. Just because we feel inferior or mess up does not mean God is done with us. I'm walking proof.

Another Chance

Approximately six years after Linda Chavez's murder, I faced a somewhat similar moment of faith. The question was, Would I fail again, or would I overcome my fears and fulfill the abundant purpose God had planned for me?

I was training employees for a business coaching contract. While the group worked through a hands-on exercise, I heard a quiet directive in my mind. *When you finish, pull Don to the side and tell him I see him, I know his thoughts, and I have told you to pray for him.*

I knew the words came from God. Yet much as it had done in that New Mexican convenience store, fear crowded my thoughts and clouded my response. *This isn't a faith-based organization. I can't do this here. And besides, I don't know if Don even believes in you.*

I felt a flash of déjà vu when God urged me, *Do it anyway.*

Linda Chavez's name immediately came to mind, sealing my decision.

At the end of the training session, I made my way through the line of people who wanted to talk about my presentation. When I finished answering the last person's questions, I nervously approached Don. "Could I speak to you privately for a moment?"

A look of curiosity crossed his face. "Yes, ma'am."

We wound our way past small groups of people bunched in discussion and walked to a quiet corner. My heart pulsed as I began, "Don, you might think I'm crazy, but I need to ask you a question. Do you believe in God?"

He brightened. "I sure do."

Relief flooded me. "So do I, Don. And a few years ago, I learned a hard lesson about listening to him and obeying when he tells me to do something. Today, he told me to pass a message on to you."

"He did?" Don's skin paled about three shades.

"He said to tell you he sees you, he knows your thoughts, and he wants me to pray for you."

I was stunned when the tall man in front of me immediately broke into the thick, ugly cry of a person unaware of anyone or anything except the power of their emotions assaulting them in that space.

Don began to stutter between breaths. "Ma'am, I haven't told anyone, not even my wife, what I've been thinking lately. My thoughts have gotten so bad, things have gone so wrong, that I've just about had it. I've seriously considered coming to work and going postal, bringing a gun and starting to shoot—then turning it on myself. "

Astounded does not adequately describe the shock I felt as I listened. It was another lesson learned about the harmful potential of worrying more about what people think versus what God asks. Thankfully, I had acted in obedience this time.

Don never did hurt anyone, including himself. I occasionally see him and when I do, he asks, "Ma'am, do you still pray for me?"

I tell him truthfully, "When God places you on my mind, I absolutely pray."

Through that incredible interaction, God lovingly gave me another chance. He could easily have given up on me and passed my purpose on to someone else.

But he didn't. And the contrast between these two lessons has taught me a great deal about living an abundant life. Speaking on a stage and writing books are not the only things I was made for. Equally important are the one-on-one interactions I have with other people, powerful moments in secluded prayer, and listening to God when he calls me to action.

Restoration

We do not know what may happen in the next minutes or hours of our day, but God does. He affirms, "Only I can tell you the future before it even happens" (Isa. 46:10).

It's reassuring to learn that even if we disobey, with repentance, God can still use us for a good more significant than ourselves. When we confess and submit to him, God loves to take our messes and use them to turn us into message bearers of his redeeming power. In Joel 2:25, he tells his people, "I will restore to you the years that the swarming locust has eaten" (NKJV).

God has restored the years of my life eaten by pain. He's not only healed my body but he's also healed my mind and emotions, strengthening me to help others.

God restored the years the locusts ate by healing my marriage in miraculous ways, allowing me to share practical and spiritual wisdom leading to happier relationships.

God restored the years the locusts ate by healing my guilty, fearful, insecure, self-loathing spirit and using me in a purposeful way, despite my former disobedience.

He is willing to do the same for you. Maybe you can't identify with the dramatic details of my story, but odds are, something big or small is hindering you from fully living the exceedingly abundant life you were made for.

Path to Peace

My experiences have taught me to release old insecurities at the foot of Jesus's cross, allowing the wholeness of his Spirit to brush away comparisons, jealousy, resentment, and divisions I previously felt toward others. His love has infused me with courage and empowered me to act in spite of fear.

For me, the path to peace was simple, though not always easy. A series of persistent action steps paved the way, helping me learn to see myself through God's eyes—freeing me to embrace all he promised. These included the following:

- Regular prayer
- Consistent Bible study
- Journaling my thoughts in letters I called "Notes to Daddy"
- Posting affirmations and Scripture around my house, in my car, and online
- Speaking forgiveness out loud to the mirror, long before I felt it

Over time, old doubts began to subside, allowing the truth that I was absolutely forgiven to seep into my soul. Today, I still think about Linda Chavez and pray for her family, but I no longer carry the weight of something I cannot change. I have allowed God to unlock the doors of my prison. I am free.

As I write this, I can't help wondering about you. Do you know God's forgiveness and acceptance? Do you trust that you're empowered? Do you truly believe your Father designed a great plan for your life? Or would you answer with one of the following?

"God couldn't forgive me."

"You don't know my circumstances."

"I'm limited by my disability or illness."

"I'm not smart, talented, or good enough."

We cannot experience the abundance of loving God and others well when we are focused on limitations or regrets. If our thoughts are consumed with past mistakes, current challenges, or perceived weaknesses, we are bound and paralyzed from fulfilling our high calling, the very reason God formed us in our mother's womb. If the majority of our mental self-talk includes complaints and self-deprecation, we need to refocus our message. We were not made for this—we were made for a more magnificent purpose.

Dare to believe God is true to his word. When he says he is willing to pardon you once you confess and repent of your wrongdoing, agree with him (Ps. 32:5). When he calls you more than a conqueror, trust that it's true (Rom. 8:31–39).

You may not believe it right now, but you are lovable, and you were made to love as well. This is one of the most intrinsic reasons you exist. The only comparison you need to make is by asking yourself, *Am I living God's best?*

Remember, God doesn't *have* to adore you; he *wants* to. Sometimes he proves it best when he gets us to himself. He wants to spend time with us. It's in his presence that he begins to whisper, "This is why I gave you breath."

MIND, BODY, AND SPIRIT STRENGTHENERS

YOUR ABUNDANT PURPOSE CHALLENGE

Stand in front of the mirror, look yourself in the eye, and dare to say, "You are acceptable, you are lovable, and you are adored. God sees you and he loves what he sees."

YOUR ABUNDANT PURPOSE EXERCISE

Go to biblegateway.com, or use a concordance you have at home, and look up the word *forgive*. Study what God says on the subject, and ask him to speak personally to you. Write down three to five specific insights.

YOUR ABUNDANT PURPOSE SCRIPTURE

Luke 10:27 (NIV): "'Love the Lord your God with all your heart and with all your soul and with all your strength and with all your mind'; and, 'Love your neighbor as yourself.'"

YOUR ABUNDANT PURPOSE PROMISE

Jesus set you free so you could experience an abundant purpose.

YOUR ABUNDANT PURPOSE STUDY AND DISCUSSION PROMPTS

Has God ever spoken personally and specifically to you from the Bible? If so, what did he say, and how did it help you?

Do you *believe* God as well as believe *in* him?

Do you believe God's promises of forgiveness, acceptance, and love are as true for you as they are for other people?

CHAPTER 3
Made for Presence

Make today worth remembering.

—Zig Ziglar, *Raising Positive Kids in a Negative World*

Tim wasn't happy. He felt like the job he used to love had turned into a nightmare.

At first, Tim thrived on the adrenaline rush triggered by tight deadlines, interviews with famous people, and breaking stories. He wasn't one of those people who'd always dreamed about working in journalism, but when a friend told him about the opening at one of the most well-known political magazines in Washington, DC, Tim jumped.

This morning, he didn't even get his jacket off before his cell phone rang. Tim cringed, knowing a five- to ten-minute conversation, no matter how important, would cause the stack on his desk to grow when he desperately needed to knock it down.

"Hey." Tim noticed how breathy his voice sounded.

"You all right?"

Tim stifled a groan. Dave was an appreciated mentor and his best friend, but he didn't have time for small talk or his friend's ability to poke the sleeping bear that Tim worked so hard to hide. He summoned energy and added it to his tone. "I'm great. Never better. Just behind as usual. I've got three research projects due today, and I need to schedule some interviews on the new tax bill everyone's buzzing about." Tim hoped his friend would hear the hint.

"Dude, you stress me out just listening to you. It worries me."

Tim turned his computer on as he spoke. "I appreciate your concern, but no need to worry. I've got everything under control." He pulled the pile of papers from his inbox.

"That's what I used to tell myself."

Tim rolled his eyes. There it was, the bear poke. He didn't want to sit through another telling of Dave's heart attack and how God used it to get his attention. "Yeah, I know. Listen, I'm sorry, but I'm really juggling a lot today. I honestly don't have time to talk."

Dave didn't answer instantly. When he did, he sounded deflated. "Busyness certainly has a way of creeping in. I feel like God's been whispering into my soul—about you."

Tim's finger stopped on the paper he was getting ready to flip over. He'd been hearing a few God whispers himself lately.

Dave continued, "Just don't get so caught up in all the busyness that you forget to notice life. It's happening all around you. Remember, why you do something is as important as what you do. And money won't replace your health. Work is a good thing, but make sure you're doing what God wants you to do. He didn't create you so you could work yourself to death."

Tim breathed a little deeper. "Thanks, Dave. I appreciate it. Let's grab breakfast this weekend."

"Text me the time and place and I'll be there."

Tim smiled and said, "Will do." He could always count on Dave.

After ending the call, Tim thought about what his friend had said while separating papers from his inbox. *Busyness has taken over. I've fallen into that category of people living to work instead of working to live. For a while now, I've felt like there has to be more to life. Days and weeks pass, and I barely realize it.*

Tim picked up a file folder to slide one of his organized stacks of papers into. But his thoughts continued while he worked. *The things that used to make me feel important now make me feel like I'm being pulled in too many directions. These days I get frustrated so easily. Surely I wasn't made to be this miserable. It isn't fair to the people I work with or to my wife and kids. God, am I doing what you want me to do? Is this all there is? Please show me what I'm missing.*

Two years would pass before Tim received an explicit answer. He would also realize how much his present situation was preparing him for the future.

A Common Struggle

Ask most people what they wish they had more of and a high percentage will list happiness in their top three. But how can you feel happy if you aren't living an abundant life? As you'll soon see, presence has everything to do with it.

What you do in this moment will determine what happens in your future. How successful you are tomorrow is being shaped by what you choose today. The abundance you seek will remain elusive if you don't wisely invest the time you are given. You are determining next year's happiness by your actions right now. The principle is straightforward.

One of the things for which I've most overreached is happiness. That elusive, compulsive, never-ending drive to feel good about breathing.

What is it in the human condition that believes we must complicate matters for things to work out? Why do we struggle to trust the simple?

The fact is, just because something is simple does not make it easy. Most of the time, happiness really is a choice, but for some reason this life-changing decision is hard for many of us to pull off.

From a personal level, I get it. Historically, as much as I've wanted to embrace my life, to worry less, to laugh more, to feel truly content, I've found it difficult to enjoy my moments. Guilt, fatigue, shame, childhood conditioning, a track record of unwanted outcomes . . . various negative impressions easily infiltrate my thinking. And statistics prove I'm not alone.

Track Your Happiness is an app developed as a scientific research project that investigates what makes life worth living by monitoring what people are doing in the moment. The original study found that people spend 46.9 percent of their time thinking about something other than what they are actually doing.[1] What does this have to do with living a purpose-filled life? I'd say everything.

Consider this—depression is grounded in brooding thoughts about the past, while anxiety is rooted in consuming thoughts about the future. The inability or refusal to focus on the present can hold us hostage and keep us from living the dreams God planted in our hearts. Instead of feeling peace and happiness, we get stuck in a rut of perceived lack.

Studies show that those who are mindful in the present, versus obsessing over the past or worrying about the future, are happier, free to be all they are meant to be. They practice what I call "Now Faith."

The New American Standard Bible presents Hebrews 11:1 this way: "*Now faith* is the assurance of things hoped for, the conviction of things not seen" (emphasis mine). Numerous other translations also start Hebrews 11:1 with the same two words: *now faith*. I believe there's a secret key for unlocking our unique purpose hidden in this consistent word choice.

Now means in this moment, at present, currently. *Faith* means believing before you see or experience an outcome. Put the two words together, and God is telling us to resolutely trust immediately—before we can see. We are to praise him for keeping his promises for an abundant life, before the results are delivered. We should bravely believe the results might even exceed what we imagine—before they are ours.

God is not stifled by season, situation, or senselessness. The only thing that restrains him is our unwillingness to believe and accept his good plan for our lives. He desires to give good things to you and me—but we must risk to receive the reward.

As I write this, I just experienced the truth of this again.

Jobette Seasons

My husband and I recently came through a long, tough period. For several years, one blindsiding wave of adversity after another knocked us off our feet like an emotional tsunami. It isn't the first time I've experienced this kind of emotional storm. I call such trials "Jobette seasons."

The term came when, during those hard times, people said I reminded them of a female Job. Early on, I wrestled with thoughts that God might have given up on me. When we were drowning in medical bills, I grappled to hold on to a thread of hope that my life had any real meaning. For years, while our son tried to rescue his child from horrific abuse and neglect, I couldn't see an extraordinary plan at work. But then, I am not God.

For my husband and me, during our greatest overwhelm, it seemed as if each time we cautiously began to get on our knees in an effort to stand back up, another wave would flatten us again. When the IRS audit letter arrived in the mail, I initially laughed; it was better than bawling. It felt like a final, cruel blow. But no matter what we've endured through the years, ultimately, God did not fail us. He proved his faithfulness.

Through those Jobette years, moment by excruciating moment, we made our way back to our feet and walked up and down valleys. We learned that though we couldn't see *how* at the time, if we grabbed God's extended hand, he would guide us through while restoring our peace.

The surprise for me came from the beauty he crafted out of those ashes. God's greatest purpose for my life was planted in pain.

In the swirl of confusion surrounding the situations we endured, I confess to questioning whether God had truly given me any special talents, gifts, or abilities. After all, how could he use someone like me with such a messed-up life?

Early on, as I got to know my heavenly Father by reading the Bible, I took note of how often he mentioned his purpose for people, or showed it by telling the true stories of those he called to do great things. They achieved the impossible and committed miraculous acts. When I compared myself to their courage, discipline, obedience, and humility, I found myself seriously lacking. Between medical bills, worry for our grandchild's life, and a host of other concerns, I confess I often focused on my fears more than on my faith.

Because of the things I'd experienced, I felt less than ordinary, definitely not worthy or able to accomplish anything special. But as I meditated on Scripture, I felt an inner conviction that I was missing something. So I did the only thing I knew to do. I prayed over the question, "God, do you have a purpose for me, and if so, will you please reveal it?"

I didn't know it yet, but he was already at work. The very difficulties we were going through were teaching me to live out faith, no matter what each moment brought, and they were preparing me to play a role in God's greater plan. The clear answer to my question came in a surprising way.

A Recurring Message

Multiple times, I heard references to the parable of the talents. The story came up in conversations with people, messages I heard in church or on the radio, in books, and even in a movie. It took a while before I finally understood that God was speaking to me.

Matthew 25:14–30 tells the story of a master who, prior to leaving on a long journey, gave each of his three servants a certain amount of money based on their abilities. Some translations call the cash "talents." Considering our purpose and what an abundant life looks like, I especially appreciate the latter term.

One servant was given five talents, and upon the master's return, presented the original amount along with five more he'd earned. The master praised him. "Well done, my good and faithful servant. You have been faithful in handling this small amount, so now I will give you many more responsibilities. Let's celebrate together" (Matt. 25:21).

The servant with the two talents also doubled his money and received the master's approval. He too was blessed with more. But the third servant . . . well, he handled things differently. He buried his single talent out of fear. Instead of investing his talent, he hid it.

The master was not pleased. He called the servant "wicked and lazy" and told him he should have at least invested with the bankers (Matt 25:26).

For over a year, I was drawn to this intriguing story. And every time

I considered the wicked and lazy servant who'd buried his talent, guilt weighed on my mind. But my question remained unanswered. If I had a talent, if God had a purpose for me, what in the world was it? His revelation caught me off guard in both timing and place.

Unearthing My Talent

I was listening to our pastor's message during church when that familiar voice interrupted my concentration. Much like he'd done in the New Mexican desert, I heard God speak into my mind.

"I gave you a talent, and you've buried it."

My heart began to pound with anticipation. "What is it?" I asked silently.

"It's right under your nose. I gave you a gift for writing."

Disappointment instantly smothered my excitement. "That's not a gift. Everyone can write."

God did not tolerate my dismissive attitude. His conviction came swiftly. "Then explain why so many people have asked you to help them with writing projects? What about the businesses who pay you to draft letters, training materials, and marketing copy? What about the kids you've helped through college by showing them how to pen essays and other assignments? How many of your friends come to you for assistance with résumés? If a gifted cook told you their talent for whipping up tasty meals wasn't special, what would you say?"

A light bulb sputtered on. "I'd tell them our greatest purpose often comes from what is so naturally wired into us that we think it's no big deal. I'd urge them to celebrate who you made them to be and to see the joy they give others as part of the abundance you designed for their life," I answered back.

"The talents I've given you deserve the same consideration. When you were a little girl contemplating your future as an adult, what did you imagine most? What did you fantasize about when you were lying beneath the clouds on summer days, or as you sat at the foot of your thinking tree? Don't you know I planted that big oak for you to dream under?"

My pulse fluttered as the memories flooded my mind. I suddenly recognized the reality of my buried truth—my special purpose existed through the passion for words God wired into me.

Before starting kindergarten, as a tiny tot, I hungered to read. In elementary school, the thing I most looked forward to was the monthly arrival of the bookmobile. I also had a geeky inner compulsion to read the dictionary for fun, searching for new words to incorporate in my conversations. At Christmas my parents could only afford a small gift or two, but I treasured the Hardy Boys and Nancy Drew books I received. Spelling bees were my forte.

And in my private moments, beneath blue skies and my massive thinking tree, I dreamed about seeing my name on a book. Someday. But because of poor choices in my teens and early adulthood, I came to believe it couldn't happen for me. I'd messed up too much.

And yet, all of these years later, as I sat in the presence of God, he was telling me that my love of words and writing were part of his special purpose. It sounded nice, but I had more questions.

"Okay, Lord, you did give me the desire to write. But I blew it. It's too late. I wasted my chances and I buried my talent. I don't have an education in journalism or creative writing. I should have started when I was younger. Plus, do you remember where I live?

"There aren't any colleges near my little town. We don't have publishing houses in this part of the country. And I don't know a soul in the industry. There's no way I could ever write for publication."

Call me crazy, but I felt God's chuckle. As clearly as anything he's ever said to me, I heard, "Am I not still God?"

Enough said.

When I got home, I told my husband that I was going to lie down for a bit. I gathered my Bible, a notebook, and a pen, and then I prayerfully began to study Matthew 25:14–30 for the umpteenth time. During this reading of the passage, however, a sentence jumped out at me like never before.

I immediately knew God was pointing it out, so I double highlighted verse 27. I do this when he tells me something of a personal and powerful nature. Then I wrote it in my notebook. "So you ought to have deposited my money with the bankers, and at my coming I would have received back my own with interest" (NKJV).

I prayed, "Lord, I know I'm the wicked and lazy servant who buried her talent. And I understand that you're telling me to dig it up. But what do I do after that? Who are the bankers? Who do you want me to invest my talents with?"

As soon as the words left my mouth, I ripped the bottom part of a page from my notebook and quickly scribbled, "Who are the bankers? Who do you want me to invest my talents with?"

Then I got up, took the paper with me, and went to my refrigerator. I placed it beneath a magnet, where it stayed. I prayed over that torn page for more than two years.

It might seem ludicrous to you that I didn't see writing as anything special, but at the time I truly did not. I had to dig down and remove a lot of dirt before God's plan was finally revealed.

I had to release my self-reproach. I had to let go of my self-loathing. I had to lay my self-recriminations at Christ's feet. Do you notice the "self" in all of this?

Before God could use me to fulfill his purpose for my life, I had to spend time in his presence, listening. I had to learn to lay my distorted self-examinations before him and to see and love myself through Christ's eyes. He taught me that godly self-analysis leads us to our special purpose—not self-hate.

This is what I've learned: our messy lives qualify us as message bearers to God's faithful commitment, Christ's enduring love, and the Holy Spirit's redeeming power. The very things I saw as obstacles were foundational to what God wanted to do in me and through me. I tell people often, "God must have always intended for me to write and speak, because he sure gave me some incredible true stories to share."

God's Plan for You

What about you? What have you buried?

Pay attention to what's taken place in your past. What childhood dreams and memories have you locked away? Ask the Holy Spirit to remind you. Don't be afraid of past mistakes or a painful history—they might be the very foundation for God's grander plan.

What's happening around you now? Are you spending time in places where you can hear God? The Bible, inspirational radio programs, faith-based movies, spiritual books, conversations with people who have a relationship with Jesus—these are all platforms he speaks from.

What is God saying to you in your daily goings-on? Is there a theme, Scripture passage, or repetitive message that keeps cropping up? If so, become attentive and listen closer. Ask him about it. Write down the questions you have and the answers he provides.

If you're going through a hard time, don't assume it puts you out of the running to make a difference in this life. Exercise Now Faith. Grip God's hand and trust him to carry you through. Let him help you navigate the trials, until he leads you into his grander plan.

I do not believe you are reading these words by accident. You are part of my unique purpose and I am part of yours. Maybe as you read this, you feel a tiny spark whispering.

"Dare to hope one more time."

"If he did it for her, maybe, just maybe . . ."

"Could God?"

"Would God?"

"For me?"

I can assure you, he is willing. He wants to do for you what he has done for others.

- You have not been so bad that God will not bless you. Ask him to forgive you and help you turn away from actions that hurt yourself and others, the things he calls sin. You are not doomed to carry a curse the rest of your life. Jesus permanently took our curses on himself and nailed them to a tree. He set you completely and permanently free from anything that made you unworthy or unqualified to live an abundant life.

- You are not too busy or underfunded. No one had more responsibilities for projects and people than the apostle Paul. Yet when he changed his focus to obeying God and allowing the Creator of time and resources to provide for all his needs, he lacked nothing. When you exercise Now Faith, God will provide.
- You are not powerless due to any circumstance, including age. Like Moses, who was eighty when he faced Pharaoh, or Mary the mother of Jesus, whose teenaged purpose altered eternity, you were made to make a difference. The power of God's Holy Spirit is available to you—simply spend time in his presence and plug into the Source.

All of this is simple. These principles lead to the remarkable life you desire; you can have happiness beyond anything you can imagine. But I won't lie, none of it is easy. About the time you think you've got it down, a new issue will force you to face yourself and fall at Jesus's feet again. The staggering news is, he never fails to meet us where we are or to turn our faith into something more amazing than we can imagine.

Speaking and Listening

In prayer we speak to God, and in Scripture God speaks to us. When you incorporate specific strategies into this intimate time in his presence, you are more likely to discover exactly what it is you were made for.

- Spend time in prayer at the beginning of your day, asking God to bless what you offer to him and other people.
- Have a notebook and pen ready. Then as you read your Bible, ask God to reveal his specific purpose for you.

- As you study God's Word, ask him to help you understand the specific abundance he desires for your life.
- Request that God would protect you from being deceived, so you don't make a choice that goes against his will for your life.
- When you come across a convicting passage in the Bible, stop and pray in repentance. (*Repent* means to turn away from.) A clear purpose requires a clear path to success.
- When a Scripture passage encourages you, praise God, then write it down. You'll need motivational and inspirational reminders on the days when pursuing your purpose gets tough.
- Brainstorm a "purpose idea list." Nothing is too crazy, costly, or cryptic for this exercise. If you think it, write it. Include dreams, abilities, things that come easy to you, passions from your childhood, any particular trait or healthy attraction that might allude to God's plan for your life. Then spend time asking him to clarify what he made you to do. Keep the list, and jot down additional insights, thoughts, and inspirations for each item as they come.
- Ponder your purpose as you go throughout your day. God is more likely to answer us when we listen attentively instead of distractedly.

And remember, you cannot unearth your true purpose if you do not consult the One who planned it.

I think that sometimes we forget what it's like to be alone with God because even when we are by ourselves, the noise of technology drowns out our senses. The computer, TV, and phone are usually all on. Few of us will drive without music so we can listen to God on the journey. We don't know what silence sounds like anymore—and therefore we can miss his voice and his plan for our lives.

Get alone in a quiet place and ask yourself these questions:

- What is it my heart beats to do?
- What will I drop everything to run to?

- What don't I mind doing?
- What makes me feel most alive in the moment?

How you answer can lead you to your abundant purpose.

Tim's Truth

A few years after Tim began inquiring of God about his job at the magazine and listening to the whispers in his spirit, he realized he was feeling drawn to do something else with his life. His wife felt the same enticement.

After their children were grown, they both went to work for a global crisis agency, entering hard-hit regions after natural disasters. Tim feels a deep satisfaction from what he does now. But he also credits his former career as an equipping place.

He said, "God used the magazine to teach me how to navigate political climates, which comes in very handy with what I do around the world today. I learned to juggle, create efficiency processes, and prioritize my time wisely. That job also taught me how to focus on God's use of the present moment to prepare us for the future, a pivotal piece in the center of chaos. I wouldn't *get* to do this if it hadn't been for what I *had* to do previously."

God was present in Tim's former job, using it to prepare him for his current mission.

Your divinely appointed purpose is likely in process already, impacting your future—preparing you to alter someone else's life. As with Moses, Mary, Paul, or even Jesus, God can use the very challenges you face to reveal a magnificent plan, far more important than you can imagine in this moment. Maybe your mundane or stress-filled job is equipping you for something else. But if you don't spend quiet time listening to God, odds are you'll never know.

Whatever your ultimate call, you must overcome your present fear before you experience your future victory.

MIND, BODY, AND SPIRIT STRENGTHENERS

YOUR ABUNDANT PURPOSE CHALLENGE

Become exceedingly intentional about faith-based gratitude. Praise God for knowing best and in advance of your future. Dare to believe before you see.

YOUR ABUNDANT PURPOSE EXERCISE

Document what and who you appreciate from every season of your life. Express your acknowledgment out loud as often as possible. If you aren't used to living real-time appreciation, it will feel awkward at first, but practice makes it easier.

YOUR ABUNDANT PURPOSE SCRIPTURE

Jeremiah 29:11 (NIV): "'For I know the plans I have for you,' declares the LORD, 'plans to prosper you and not to harm you, plans to give you hope and a future.'"

YOUR ABUNDANT PURPOSE PROMISE

God built talents, gifts, and special abilities into you when he handcrafted you in your mother's womb.

YOUR ABUNDANT PURPOSE STUDY AND DISCUSSION PROMPTS

Do you allow yourself to sit in silence, or do you surround yourself with noise to cover the discomfort of what God might say if you were still and listened?

What has God been whispering to you?

Why do you think things like Now Faith, focusing on what's happening in the moment, and seeing the current blessings in our hands are so difficult?

CHAPTER 4
Made for Courage

Courage is found in unlikely places.
—J. R. R. Tolkien, *The Fellowship of the Ring*

The deadline for this book is looming, some heavy-duty prayer requests are pouring in, I just lost someone who felt like family, I need to prepare a speaking presentation, friends are disappointed that I'm not available, and I'm battling insecurity over what I write. I feel overwhelmed and afraid. I'm familiar with healthy fear, the kind that drives us to act when we would otherwise remain stagnant. But the fear I'm dealing with is far from healthy. If I listened to my feelings in this moment, I'd throw my hands up in defeat.

But if God made me to write, speak, and pray for others—as he's confirmed many times—then giving in to the kind of fear that drives procrastination is not an option. I could miss out on the joy of fulfilling my God-given purpose.

I'm guessing that you can identify with my struggle. Have you ever received a God-nudge to act on, followed by the immediate gut kick of fear?

Whether it's picking up the phone and calling a friend, visiting someone who is in the hospital or a nursing home, taking responsibility for hurting someone else, or researching how to pursue that dream you've tucked away, you have likely felt prompted to do something. Beating back fear is difficult, but an ongoing wrestling match with guilt is even worse.

Taking Courage

Unhealthy fear is the opposite of courage. Fear is an emotion you feel; courage is an action you take. We are made for the latter. We are called to live an abundantly brave life, to rise above our fears and act with resolute courage. The Bible tells us so.

Many times in Scripture, God tells his people to "take courage." He understands our emotional battles. If you want to do an interesting study, search "do not fear" and "take courage" in a Bible app or on biblegateway.com and see what you learn. Check across translations. Read full passages to understand the context and why people were given this instruction. Ask yourself how this might pertain to the God-nudges you sense.

According to *Merriam-Webster*, of the many definitions for the word *take*, some include "to seize or capture," "choose," and "lay hold."[1] *Courage* is defined as "mental or moral strength to venture, persevere, and withstand danger, fear, or difficulty."[2]

To take courage requires action. Think about what these words might represent for you. Are there fears you need to overcome? Faith you need to exercise? Fortitude you need to choose so you can fully explore your purpose and destiny?

For instance, I'm writing this now because I took action in spite of how I felt. I bravely picked up my computer and began to type—though I worried my words might fall short.

One thing is definite: if I didn't type at all, I would reach no one with this message. But by my attempting, at least one person might benefit.

Like me, you have been commissioned by God with a unique purpose. I dare you to believe.

There comes a point when you must stop rationalizing, excusing, and justifying. Be brutally honest with yourself: Are you doing all you can do in order to be all you are meant to be?

Nothing improves until we admit to ourselves that something is wrong—and nothing is more wrong than when we are not living the abundant life we were made for.

In my case, I almost missed the chance to do what I was made for because of fear, pain, and doubt. But two questions burned in my soul and helped me move past my emotions.

Two Revealing Questions

Consider the following:

- How will I feel if my entire life passes and I reach the end wondering, *What if?*
- What's the worst thing that can happen if I try and fail?

In my case, it seemed crazy to make an attempt as a professional writer. But now I know the answer to my what-if.

When I prayed over the questions on my refrigerator (*Who are the bankers? Who do you want me to invest my talents with?),* I admit there were days I wondered if I was wasting my breath. After all, I'd misused a lot of years, and I felt like I had no more time to squander. It made sense that God had probably given up on me, as I'd given up on myself. Surely, if he wanted me to write professionally, he would have already made something happen. And it wasn't like I didn't get any answer at all; I simply didn't like what I heard.

I think Psalm 46:10 is one of the most challenging Scripture verses in the whole Bible: "Be still, and know that I am God" (NIV). In my search for purpose, I was looking for something a bit more concrete.

When you are eager to learn God's specific plan for your life, "be still" is not an encouraging message. However, with absolutely no idea how to proceed, the only recourse is to wait and obey until God decides to give you more direction. When he does, sometimes you must press through awkward and uncomfortable situations in order to receive his full disclosure.

As I share my experience, perhaps you can recall times you wondered why you had to endure trying circumstances when your heart's cry was simply to obey God and be what he wanted for you. Maybe you are sitting in that exact place right now. If so, hold on to your faith, know that God is listening, and even when you can't see any sign of movement, trust that he is preparing and equipping you for things yet to be revealed.

For me, after praying, listening, and being forced to be still for a season, God divulged the occasion for my next faith step in a surprising way.

I was out of state, sitting in the back of a room at a training certification course, embarrassed and humiliated. For three days I'd hacked and coughed, and my nose ran like water through a sieve. Though it was June in Texas, I looked and sounded like I had a December flu in Alaska. I desperately tried to smother the gross sounds of my uncontrollable bodily functions, but my attempts were mostly futile. Several times, I wondered if I should just pack up and leave, but I felt a compulsion to stay.

Thankfully, the other attendees were compassionate, but I still felt discouraged.

During the last break before the final session, I stepped outside into the muggy Texas heat. The radiating effect seeped into my bones and warmed my chilly insides. I walked past the building and down a sidewalk, head down, feeling sorry for myself.

I'd ventured a couple of blocks when I looked up to see what lay ahead. Directly in front of me, a few feet away, stood a tree shaped in a perfect Y. The significance broke me.

I looked skyward and said to God, "Exactly. Why? Why am I so sick? Why is this happening? Why am I even here?"

Traffic and chirping birds were my only answer. God was silent. I turned on my heels and headed back inside.

As soon as I sat down, someone came around and passed out cards. I scanned the script multiple times, to ensure I wasn't seeing a mirage. "Have you ever wanted to write? Speaking and writing go hand in glove. Join us in Glorieta, New Mexico, for our writer's conference, October 22–26, 2008."

I don't remember if I even sniffled again.

One of the other attendees leaned close. "You should go. I am. I've attended the past few years, and it's a great conference."

I wanted to hug her but was afraid of passing my germs.

Within an hour I was registered. But the moment I pushed the submit button, I regretted it.

Anxiety grabbed my gut. What had I done? I didn't know any writers.

I wrestled with myself for days. Should I call and cancel my registration? But I came to a defining conclusion. I was tired of living in fear—I'd done it all my life. This time I resolved to take courage, act in faith, and invest with the bankers God had sent. It didn't matter whether the return on my investment came in the form of writing for publication or simply so I could pass on a legacy of stories and lessons to my family. I determined to see it through.

Four months later, I boarded a plane alone and flew to New Mexico. My insides quaked, but I'd taken the first step toward living out a plan much bigger than anything I ever dreamed. However, fear followed me to the conference. Satan didn't want me to pursue my purpose, so I needed to find a way to protect myself against his persistent lies.

Can you relate to the fears and lies that hold a person back? Reflect on your dreams, passions, and desires. Consider your purpose. What have you buried, and how can you unearth it? I assure you, it's not too late.

The Key to Choosing Abundance

In John 10:10, Jesus said, "The thief does not come except to steal, and to kill, and to destroy. I have come that they may have life, and that they may have it more abundantly" (NKJV).

What is the *it* in this passage? Life. And what kind of life did Jesus come to give us? An overflowing one—but we have to push unhealthy fears aside, or they will steal, kill, and destroy what we are made for through emotional paralysis.

If you're anything like me, when the enemy sends unhealthy fear, you need a mental reset. The following may help move you quicker to the abundant life Christ promised.

- What's not good enough in your life? Do you feel energized and alive? If not, what can you do to change either your situation or your view of the situation?
- What frustrates or concerns you about your life? What can you do to overcome those frustrations and concerns?
- Envision the pleasure you would feel if you achieved the longings you've buried. Close your eyes, and truly let yourself see, hear, feel, taste, and smell what you could experience.
- Challenge yourself. What am I truly committed to and why? What really matters to me? Assess your answers honestly. And remember, where you spend your time, energy, and money will reveal the truth.
- Ask God to show you the talents you've buried and reveal to you where he wants you to invest them.
- What if God has an extraordinary plan for your life, and you're allowing the comfort of your current conditions to rob you of the "more" you were made for?
- What if, step by intentional step, you could prepare, educate yourself, and progress toward fulfilling your purpose?
- What if your whole life passed you by, leaving you to wonder if you might have achieved the dreams God planted inside you but never knowing?
- What if the challenges you face today are designed by God to teach and strengthen you to accomplish a greater good, regardless of how Satan tries to convince you otherwise? Remember, Satan fights against us most when we're right where God wants us to be.

When you feel afraid, that's the best time to exercise bravery. Courage is only necessary when there is something to lose and something to gain.

When you submit to God's plans, everything you experience will be used to fulfill his purpose for you. I know this full well.

Becoming One of the "One"

I can't recall whether it was the first or second session at the writer's conference when my dream burst. About forty of us were squeezed into a room that reminded me of my high school science class. My notebook was open and my pen poised. I was ready to learn how to fulfill God's calling on my life. But the first words I heard made my hand fall.

The speaker, a tall, dark-haired man with eyes to match, stood at the front of the room and cleared his throat. "I don't mean to discourage anyone, but I feel I need to be honest. Only about 1 percent of aspiring authors ever succeed in getting published by a royalty house publisher—where they pay you, instead of you paying them to print your books."

A part of me thought, *Well, I'll just write for my family.* And I could have accepted it if that was the entirety of God's plan for me.

But another side of my brain couldn't come to terms with the situation. *Wait, I spent a lot of money to get here. I used my vacation time from work. Aren't these the bankers I'm supposed to invest my talents with? What about my years of prayer and seeking?*

I scanned the room to peek at people. A few looked as stricken and scared as I felt, but in my estimation, most looked much more assured and capable than I did.

The instructor spoke again. "Most aspiring authors don't succeed because 99 percent give up. Writing is not a magical process; it's a matter of persistent hard work."

It made me think of the Thomas Edison quote, "Genius is 1 percent inspiration and 99 percent perspiration."

Hard work? I could do hard work. The tone of my conversation with God immediately changed. *Lord, if you want me to do this, show me how to become one of the 1 percent.*

During the rest of the conference, I got up early to make sure I didn't miss a class and absorbed every bit of knowledge I could gather. I feverishly took notes in each session. I sat up late, sipping steaming lattes, while I talked to other conferees, learning from those who were further along on the quest for publication. By the end, I was on an emotional high, especially after a conversation with a book publisher ended with him calling out, "Get me that proposal."

When I told a few new writing friends about the exchange, I caught their contagious enthusiasm and rode that high through the conference. Adrenaline rushed through my veins, because I had harnessed my fear and seen God come through. The thrill lasted onto my plane ride home, when I realized something very important. I had no idea how to write a book proposal.

Resolve and Faith

Have you ever languished in procrastination due to unhealthy fear magnified by guilt?

A few days after I arrived home, I was sitting in my office, stewing over my dilemma. An amazing opportunity was at my fingertips, but I had no idea what to do with it. Maybe I needed to give up before I got in too deep. What if I made a fool of myself?

But then I prayed, *Lord, show me how to become one of the 1 percent. Where do you want me to invest my talents?* I waited in silence.

An idea popped into my head. *Set a goal.*

A plan began to formulate. I decided to read one hundred books on the craft and business of writing. I don't know why I decided on one hundred, but that was the number I chose. I wrote down the goal, along with a deadline to meet it, and emailed my intention to a friend. Studies have shown that putting things in black-and-white drives our subconscious minds to complete what we want to achieve.

I went to the library and visited bookstores to find good information on writing. I soon needed a bookcase to house my resources, but I was getting quite an education. And I practiced while I learned.

It took me just over eighteen months, but I did it. And with that accomplishment, I had not just one but two completed book proposals in hand. I'd faced down my fear and honed my raw talent. I was ready to invest with the next banker.

I've never regretted my decision to act in spite of the fears I felt, but I would have regretted not taking the chance.

Make no mistake, those what-ifs will eat you up. Unearthing your talent requires resolve. Faith in God's plan for the ultimate outcome will help you fulfill your call. Whether success manifests itself publicly or privately, your greatest sense of purpose will come from obedience. So what's your story?

Writing is part of my incredible purpose, but what is yours? What have you secretly wanted to do but never believed in yourself enough to chance? What is tugging at your spirit, calling you to try? What is pulling you back, making you terrified of failing? What makes jealousy rise in you because you see others doing something you wish you could do? What opportunities are available to you that you are afraid of acting on?

A Surefire Strategy for Overcoming Challenges

In the subtitle of this book, I promised you spiritual strategies to help you unearth your own abundant purpose. I intend to keep my word.

So far, I've bared my soul so you can see this is not what I call a stuff-and-fluff message. I understand the confusion, questions, and concerns that surround a person's existence. Why *do* we exist? How can we be such messes and still make a meaningful difference?

Two lessons have steadied me when challenges hit. Maybe they will help you.

1. You cannot trust your emotions when everything around you seems to spin out of control. Situations are not always as they appear. And Satan will try to use your fears to stop you from fulfilling your purpose.
2. What you focus on in the moment can determine your future.

I learned these truths through hard adversities. When the going gets tough, I go to the Bible. Documented evidence of God's provision gives me hope. This surefire strategy has become a natural skill, righting my world when it feels upside down.

Recently, I had the privilege of reminding a brilliant and beautiful young woman of this fact. She did not see her own potential. She was temporarily blinded, prevented from seeing God's intentions for her life. I understood all too well.

Her early morning text read, "I can't do this! I've been up all night having one panic attack after another. I'm too scared to go for my interview. But I'm scared to call and tell them I'm not coming in. What do I do?"

It didn't require much thought for me to offer her encouragement. I texted right back:

> You CAN do this!!!
>
> Here's what I want you to remember:
>
> Consider Daniel in the den. Don't you think he faced terror and anxiety when his enemies cast him into a pit full of starving lions? Think of him as a real person, not the bigger-than-life character we've made him out to be. What if Daniel had turned his back on all of the opportunities God gave him to step out in faith? Not only would he have missed out on a whole lot of blessings but we would have missed out on his inspiration!
>
> What about Ruth? If she had stayed paralyzed where she was, she would have missed out on the beautiful husband God had waiting for her in her new place. And we wouldn't have Jesus, because in the book of Matthew, she is listed in his lineage.
>
> Consider Jesus himself. Talk about anxiety. He sweated great drops of blood as he steeled himself to go

> through a change in life none of us could imagine. And yet . . . what if he had backed out? Where would we be?
>
> The Bible is full of terrified, anxious, depressed people called by God to move from where they were so he could use them to do something far greater than themselves! Satan wants you to give in to the fear because he knows the talents and traits God built into you to do exceedingly more than you can conceive. Do not give him the satisfaction of defeating you before you start.
>
> Instead, do what God is calling you to do. Step out in faith, do it scared, and let him carry you to far more amazing things than you could think or imagine to ask for. This is your day. Let the joy of the Lord be your strength! Jesus promised you an amazing life—it's yours, if you only choose to accept it!

It was the motivational pep talk my young friend needed, and it gave her the courage to seize the opportunity in front of her. But our exchange also did something for me. It provided one more beautiful example of how God had redeemed my past pain and transformed it into something inspirational. It filled me with a renewed sense of my own special purpose.

Had I not endured some agonizing events, I would have nothing of substance to offer. While I writhed in gut-wrenching sorrow, I couldn't imagine feeling like I do today. But God saw ahead in time to what he wanted to do through me. No adversity is ever wasted unless we overlook opportunities to use it for something good.

I want to offer you encouragement similar to what I gave my young friend. You were made for something very special. God is able to do exceedingly more in your life than you can think or imagine to ask (Eph. 3:20). He made you for more than worry, stress, frazzled nerves, fear, or a lack mentality.

As we continue, we'll explore various callings and vocations, skills and strategies, as well as other true stories. Through the process, ask yourself, "What was I created for? How is my life meant to impact others? What brings me true joy?"

Be assured, you were made to do more than inhale air, even if it doesn't feel like it right now.

What abilities, talents, resources, or gifts are in your hands today? In faith, offer them to Jesus, even if you think they aren't special. Then through his power, stand back and watch what he will do.

MIND, BODY, AND SPIRIT STRENGTHENERS

YOUR ABUNDANT PURPOSE CHALLENGE

Most of us start with big dreams, but we forget it often takes small steps to achieve them. As a speaker, I started with one person at a time, then spoke to groups of twenty-five or fewer. Eventually, that number grew to more than one hundred, until finally thousands sat in some of my audiences. Remember to exercise patience while you move toward fulfilling your purpose. Ask yourself, "What is the next best step I should take?"

YOUR ABUNDANT PURPOSE EXERCISE

Any time you pursue a purpose, naysayers will rise to the occasion, spouting pessimism and doubt. Ask God about your dreams. If he is calling you to action, refuse to repeat a destroyer's words to yourself—refute them by writing down God's promises and keeping them close.

YOUR ABUNDANT PURPOSE SCRIPTURE

Jeremiah 33:3: "Ask me and I will tell you remarkable secrets you do not know about things to come."

YOUR ABUNDANT PURPOSE PROMISE

No fear can prevail when you take courage.

YOUR ABUNDANT PURPOSE STUDY AND DISCUSSION PROMPTS

What are the fears you battle most often? Are they the kind of fears that inspire and motivate you, or do they stifle and strangle your dreams? What are some ways you can battle your unhealthy fears today?

At your life's end, will your current decisions lead to results or regrets?

What has helped you make it through painful circumstances? Could others benefit from what you've learned? Could you influence changes that would protect others from having to face what you've undergone? What good could you initiate as a result of that pain?

CHAPTER 5

Made for Play

This does not mean that we are to be perpetually solemn. We must play.

—C. S. Lewis, *The Weight of Glory*

Spend fifteen minutes in the presence of children at play and tell me their joy isn't contagious. The company of laughing adults is much more pleasant than somber ones. When you see a married couple giggling together, don't you think, *I want that*?

I wanted to address the topic of play early in this book. Why? Because if you are going to unearth your abundant purpose or even make an attempt to do so, the balance of playful moments will sustain you and give you the strength you need. Even Nehemiah, one of the hardest working men in the whole Bible, prescribed appropriate times of relaxation and celebration. He said, "The joy of the LORD is your strength" (Neh. 8:10).

We often forget that God designed us for laughter, enjoyment, and healthy pleasure as well as for seriousness, discipline, and hard toil. Throughout Scripture, God's people who endured so much also enjoyed times of refreshment through appointed feasts and festivals by God's command.

In today's society, many people excel in work and worry but fail at rest and relaxation. To see your dreams through, you will need endurance. Laughter, joy, and play produce positive energy—necessary if you want to finish what you start.

A Motivating Factor

Merriam-Webster describes *play* as, among other defining qualities, "recreational activity; *especially:* the spontaneous activity of children," and "absence of serious or harmful intent."[1]

These descriptions remind me that playfulness has helped me work through many of the dull, boring, and monotonous steps on the way to achieving my dreams. I learned how to use play to my advantage from my kids.

When my sons were small, bedtime preparation often started out rough. I would tell them to pick up their toys, and they would grumble, procrastinate, and sometimes even try to hide. They would do anything to get out of that chore—until I started our game.

"I'll bet I can pick up more toys faster than you," I would challenge. Then I'd scurry to scoop up a handful of trucks, cars, and LEGOs. "One . . . two . . . three . . . you can't beat me."

In lightning-like fashion, they rushed to snatch a pile of their own, counting their toys like I did. I loved hearing them say, "I win, Mommy." Their bodies bounced around the room with their giggles, as toy after toy dropped in the box.

Each time was the same. We went back and forth for only a few minutes, laughing and learning together. Not only did we clean up the room in a flash, but I was training my children to count as well as to enjoy the accomplishment of a job well done. Those are still some of my most treasured moments from their childhoods.

If you have children or grandchildren and you've ever played this game, you know what I mean. But have you ever thought about what this game can teach adults? Children are great models to observe.

All you have to do is watch an innocent child, and in a short amount of time you will see how powerfully imagination, games, and play alter their attitude. Take almost any kid who is cranky about a project, make a game out of it, and watch that boy's or girl's mood shift. Not only will the job get done, but usually the child will do it faster and better. I still use this tactic with children, but I also use this strategy on someone else—me.

I motivate myself in many ways. Sometimes I use time challenges, racing against the clock to see how speedily and accurately I can accomplish a task.

Occasionally I imagine myself going up against, or working alongside, a person who's achieved something I desire, and it's game on. Can I do things as well as or better than them? What would I do differently? What would I do the same? If we teamed up on our efforts, what creative concepts could we produce?

Often I tell myself, *Just work on it for fifteen minutes, then you can quit.* I almost always keep going once I've gained momentum, and even though I know it's a mental exercise, the psychology still sets me in motion.

One of my most dramatic personal mind games is to imagine I have only ninety days to live. What would I want to finish that I've already started? What would I regret or feel embarrassed I didn't achieve? What would make me feel good about the life I've lived? What legacy or imprint do I want to leave?

I've spent time in the presence of people who were dying and knew it. As I've listened to their memories, concerns, and regrets, one blaring consistency stands out. Not one man or woman has ever complained they spent too much time laughing or smiling. No one has told me they wished they hadn't pursued their inner interests with the excitement of a child. Nor has someone said, "I wish I hadn't hung out with family and friends so much." When reviewing their life, not a single individual has expressed angst over the moments they let themselves relax and unwind. Instead, the opposite is true.

To a person, I've heard remorse over too much energy spent on criticism and not enough celebration. Overemphasis on seriousness with an underemphasis on lightheartedness has haunted many to their final breath. Some wished they'd followed their childhood desires with childlike delight. Most mourned missed opportunities to enjoy their loved ones.

Parents wished they'd scheduled more playdates with their kids. Spouses wish they'd written more honey-go lists versus honey-do lists, putting playtimes on their calendars. People wanted one more chance to hang out with their friends.

I believe part of any human being's exceedingly abundant purpose is to enjoy the life and people they've been given. God did create moments to laugh as well as to weep (Eccl. 3:4). The former can help us survive the latter—particularly when we are pursuing the aspirations that drive us.

What about your dreams? The next time you feel tired, bored, or ready to quit, try challenging yourself with one or more of these mental games. The results will likely encourage as well as surprise you. Like children, we adults are more pleasant to be around, and often work faster and better, when we add a little play to our process. And childlike imagination is one of the more motivating factors you can use to help you achieve your goals.

Close your eyes and imagine yourself in heaven. You're standing in a room full of boxes wrapped in sparkling paper and beautiful bows. When you inquire about their meaning, your attention is directed to the label affixed to the top of each. One, a perfect square dressed in purple shimmer, says *Purpose*. A shining red one reads *Risks*. A blue box glitters, highlighting the word *Dreams*. A gleaming green octagon says *Talents*. And an oblong silver box glistens, reflecting the word *Play*. These packages represent the pile of missed opportunities we can accumulate if we don't make the most of every moment we are given.

Remember, the worst that can happen is not failure; it's not attempting at all. One of the best gifts we can give ourselves is refusing to allow the worries of this world to hinder our call.

A Remedy for Stress

Why do we fool ourselves into thinking we are more effective or spiritual if we teeter on the edge of exhaustion? A God-honoring life is something we should take seriously, but if we aren't careful, our zeal can drain us physically, emotionally, and spiritually.

There's a reason why the Bible tells us "a cheerful heart is good medicine" (Prov. 17:22). Playfulness is a great remedy for stress. An effective tension reliever comes from enjoyable interactions with people, especially when our mind-set is purposed to create and look for the joy. Play generates pleasure and happiness, making us more attractive to others—who wants to be around a chronic complainer or sour person? You can prescribe your own remedy for stress when you release worry, frustration, disappointment, fear, or any negative focus through deliberately playful moments. Contribute to someone else's relaxation and you can free your own spirit from mental weights.

The word *recreation*, another form of the word *play*, originates from the terms *re-create* or *renew*. Our energy resurges and our creativity restarts when we set aside time to rest and play. We cannot fulfill our unique purpose without recharging our batteries when they get low—and a few chuckles can provide a booster.

The following short story, told to me by an old farmer who has now passed on, is a great example of how God might laugh with us. The farmer's stress-relieving tale goes like this.

On the first day, God created the dog and said, "Sit all day by the door of your house and bark at anyone who comes in or walks past. For this, I will give you a life span of twenty years."

The dog said, "That's a long time to bark. How about only ten years and I'll give you back the other ten? Deal?"

So God agreed with the dog.

On the second day, God created the monkey and said, "Entertain people. Do tricks and make them laugh. For this, I'll give you a twenty-year life span."

The monkey said, "Monkey tricks for twenty years? That's a pretty long time to perform. How about I give you back ten like the dog?"

And God agreed with the monkey.

On the third day, God created the cow and said, "You must go into the field with the farmer all day long and suffer under the sun, have calves, and give milk to support the farmer's family. For this, I will give you a life span of sixty years."

The cow said, "That sounds like a tough life. You want me to live for sixty years? How about twenty, and I'll give you back the other forty?"

God agreed again.

On the fourth day, God created man and said, "Eat, sleep, play, marry, and enjoy your life. For this, I'll give you twenty years."

But man responded, "Only twenty years? Could you possibly give me my twenty, the forty the cow gave back, the ten the monkey returned, and the ten the dog refused? That makes eighty. Okay?"

God said, "You asked for it."

So that is why the first twenty years we eat, sleep, play, and enjoy ourselves. For the next forty, we slave in the sun to support our families. During the next ten years, we do monkey tricks to entertain the grandchildren. And for the last ten, we sit on the front porch and bark at everyone.

A Playful Plan

Though the close-to-home reflections in the previous story make it funny, and the giggle can do us good, the timeline may be off. Regardless of what stage of life we're in, when our fun-meter gets broken, we all tend to bark. Perhaps you will relate to the feelings my friend Tara recently expressed on Facebook. She wrote:

> This week has been tough on me . . . the fact that I've not been able to make it to the gym has me down, too. Adulting is hard . . . yeah, yeah.
>
> Here are my thoughts. I'm a failure. It hurts. I'm hard on my kids and then second-guess myself. I hold them accountable for a lot of things other parents don't. Then I always have a twinge of guilt. The way I see it, they need to learn certain things, it's easier now, than

> it would be later. On top of that, I can't do it all, and certainly shouldn't have to.
>
> This morning when I was taking three of them to summer school, we were jamming to the music, and I joyfully said, "Let's start our day with Jesus in our hearts, be nice, show love, forgive those who hurt you!" They thought I was a little nutty, (I was dancing in my seat), but they happily joined in.
>
> Sounds great, right? Here's my problem. If I know this is what we should do, why is it so hard for me to take my own advice? I don't get it. I've had a very rough day and week, and I need Jesus. In my heart, in my actions, in my very fiber! All. Day. Long!

Tara, like me and maybe like you, sometimes fights to feel "enough"—the antithesis of what fuels us to fulfill our abundant purpose. It sounds like her fun-meter was broken or at least temporarily down.

Discouragement ultimately visits us all. But just because we feel it doesn't mean we must wallow there. I appreciate Tara's transparency, and I like her attitude. We can all learn from what she displayed.

Sure, "adulting" is hard. Yes, we sometimes feel less-than. But we can get through anything when we admit our need for Jesus and allow ourselves to play. Even if it's nothing more than making a joyful noise in the car and dancing in the seats.

Whatever you are called to do, do it joyfully, as much as you can. When you can't, take a break and refuel, repair your fun-meter, ask God to restore the childlike playfulness inside you. You're going to need it if you want to live a full life of abundance for the long haul. It's all right to enjoy downtime with family and friends, and personally, I think it's okay to occasionally get out and play with Jesus.

By now I've given you a pretty intimate look inside my life, so I hope you'll understand the context of what I'm about to share. Please realize how seriously I take my relationship with my Savior. I strive to honor him in all I do, even when I invite him to play.

I mostly listen to contemporary Christian music these days, as I told Troy Gentry when we met at the country music festival. However, one of the secrets I employ for repairing my fun-meter is to occasionally turn on a carefully chosen classic song, tweak the words as needed, and make it into a love song of worship between my Creator and me. Choosing music from my youth revives me, and it intensifies my sense of intimacy with Christ.

Alone in my car or house, I let loose and sing loudly. But a word of caution: if you try this yourself, make sure the windows are closed, especially if your voice cracks or you sing off-key—as I can when I belt it out. I've embarrassed myself a time or two sitting at a stoplight, when I forgot the window was down.

A few of my favorite choices include, "I'm a Believer" by the Monkees, "How Deep Is Your Love" by the Bee Gees, and "The Fighter" by Keith Urban and Carrie Underwood. It isn't the song that matters, it's about the heart with which I sing to Jesus and the happiness it instills inside my soul.

What about you? When was the last time you laughed—really belly-rolled? When was the last time you let your hair down and enjoyed your time with Jesus? When was the last time you allowed yourself some healthy play? How long has it been since you took pleasure in the activities you enjoyed as a child?

Climb a tree, lay in the grass, roll down a hill, play kickball, color, pretend to be a superhero, find something that refreshes you. Silliness is a great invigorator.

I imagine God takes great pleasure in watching his children enjoy the life he's given them. Maybe that's why Zephaniah 3:17 states, "The Lord your God is living among you. He is a mighty savior. He will take delight in you with gladness. With his love, he will calm all your fears. He will rejoice over you with joyful songs."

No matter what dream you're chasing or what God has called you to, go after it with enthusiasm—and refill yourself along the way. Like you might with a child, challenge yourself and make even the mundane interesting by incorporating games. Consider what you might miss if you don't make the most of your minutes. Dare to laugh and play with Jesus. Celebrate the exceedingly abundant life you've been given. Dare to live joyfully in the process of fulfilling your special purpose. This is part of his plan—as is his desire that you not do life alone.

MIND, BODY, AND SPIRIT STRENGTHENERS

YOUR ABUNDANT PURPOSE CHALLENGE

Compete with yourself and against statistics to measure small achievements on your way to fulfilling God's grander plan. Make a game out of the difficult and tedious.

YOUR ABUNDANT PURPOSE EXERCISE

Schedule playdates and put them on your calendar. Don't fail to celebrate your successes with those you love.

YOUR ABUNDANT PURPOSE SCRIPTURE

1 Timothy 6:17 (NASB): "Instruct those who are rich in this present world not to be conceited or to fix their hope on the uncertainty of riches, but on God, who richly supplies us with all things to enjoy."

YOUR ABUNDANT PURPOSE PROMISE

Laughter was designed by God—it's good for us to smile.

YOUR ABUNDANT PURPOSE STUDY AND DISCUSSION PROMPTS

When was the last time you allowed yourself true enjoyment? The kind of childlike play or rolling-on-the-floor laughter that lifted your spirits and energized your soul? If it wasn't recently, what is holding you back?

What healthy recreation or amusement have you not participated in for a long time? Why did you stop? What's preventing you from starting again?

Why do so many believers walk around like their fun-meter is broken? What kind of message do we display when this happens?

CHAPTER 6
Made for Relationship

Love like there's no tomorrow, and if tomorrow comes, love again.
—Max Lucado, *Great Day Every Day*

The Harvard Study of Adult Development is one of the longest running examinations of adult life, marking its eightieth year in 2018. Researchers hoped to discover clues leading to healthy and happy lives, but they found more than they expected. Robert Waldinger, a professor of psychiatry at Harvard Medical School and the director of the study at the time of this writing, told the *Harvard Gazette*, "The surprising finding is that our relationships and how happy we are in our relationships has a powerful influence on our health. . . . Taking care of your body is important, but tending to your relationships is a form of self-care too."[1]

According to the study, close relationships—far more than big positions, fat bank accounts, social class, IQ, DNA, or any other conditions—have made people happy throughout their lives. Research proves the ties that bind protect people from mental and physical decline.

In his popular TED Talk, "What Makes a Good Life?" Waldinger said, "The people who were the most satisfied in their relationships at age fifty were the healthiest at age eighty."[2] And as reported in the *Harvard Gazette*, "Those who kept warm relationships lived longer and happier, . . . and the loners often died earlier. 'Loneliness kills,' he said. 'It's as powerful as smoking or alcoholism.'"

I would define it this way: a truly abundant life includes strong relationships. But in our twenty-first-century society, this flies in the face of many people's behavioral habits. We have more access to communication resources than any other generation in history, but I'm afraid we are connecting, talking, and listening less than ever before.

Most people rarely reach beyond surface contact, missing out on vital relationships, necessary if we want to accomplish a goal. And using people for selfish gain does not count. However, sacrificial giving often provides more than you might imagine.

Making Yourself Available

His name was Laszlo, and I met him at a church. He towered over me—I'd guess his height around six foot four. He had beautiful slate-gray irises and silver hair, a thick Hungarian accent, and an initially intimidating demeanor. He held my eyes in an unwavering stare and gripped my hand hard when we shook. His story, however, held intrigue. Laszlo was a Holocaust survivor.

We quickly struck up a strange friendship, and for several months, I drove to his hometown, where we met once a week. He wanted to tell his story, and he allowed me to record our visits so I could write about him. Laszlo was almost eighty when we met, and he died before we finished his interviews. Until this moment, I have not publicly shared any part of our conversations, but the following event ties perfectly with this book's message. The power of relationship often serves a larger purpose.

Laszlo said, "I was a young man when they herded us onto the cattle cars. We were piled in by the thousands, not knowing where they were taking us. It was a prison camp called Auschwitz."

Laszlo's brows furrowed. "The winds were frigid at the time of my captivity. When they pulled us from our homes, we were not given the opportunity to put on a coat or a hat. They just took us. I was one of the lucky ones—at least I had shoes on my feet."

He took a sip of his soda; Dr Pepper was Laszlo's favorite. Then he continued. "The temperatures dropped as night fell, and snow blew through the slats in the train cars. No one spoke. Few made eye contact. Everyone was scared and guarded, so most kept to themselves. Every man was protecting himself—except one.

"I do not know what his name was, I had seen him in the market before we were taken, but he was a stranger. He had kind eyes, and he urged us to huddle together to keep warm, but many refused. The ones who listened, though—well, they awoke in the morning. The rest, they did not. People of all ages had frozen in the night. Again, I was one of the lucky ones."

In typical Laszlo style, he leaned close and spoke passionately. "People must know: there is no stranger when need prevails. Pride will take your life. We need people, or we will die in the night."

Laszlo's experience makes the point. Whether physically, emotionally, financially, or metaphorically, loneliness does kill. We need people. Part of our purpose on this planet is to live in relationship, showing kindness not only to those we know but to strangers as well.

You are likely not starving, but what can you offer those who are? You probably have a roof over your head, but how can you help those who don't? Odds are you have a job, but who do you know who needs a foot in the door?

By sharing space and body heat, Laszlo survived what many did not. His story should motivate all of us. Not only did he help save others, but by making himself available, he allowed others to save him. It wasn't until Laszlo's death that I realized my meetings with him furthered that point.

Too often in today's harried and hurried culture, the elderly are treated as if they are relics of the past, with no place or purpose in the present. But if we rush past them, treating the men and women who came before us as if they are invisible or a nuisance, we will miss opportunities both to give and to receive.

It wasn't always easy to carve out the time for my visits with Laszlo, but when I saw his face light up, I was always glad I did. In hindsight, I realize our meetings gave him something to look forward to. By offering a listening ear and caring heart, I gave Laszlo the gift of feeling important. Recording his stories with the hope of sharing them with the world provided him with a sense of lasting value—beyond life on this earth. And I received much in return.

Laszlo's wisdom helped me look at circumstances through a different lens. He is one of the people God sent to teach me priceless lessons. Laszlo encouraged me to look beyond the present and consider consequences—potential good and bad—helping me make better choices. He taught me to open up my heart and allow others in, assuring me the rewards were worth any risks. He often said, "The cost of vulnerability is low compared to what you will receive."

Laszlo reminded me to look for and express gratitude in all things—especially when life took unexpected turns. And the passionate Holocaust survivor especially preached the importance of not trying to handle difficulties by yourself.

There's nothing wrong with being in survival mode when circumstances necessitate, but as Laszlo said, "Don't make the mistake of trying to go it alone." Not only do we find strength by bonding through relationship, but often we discover that the solutions to our problems lie in the hands of others.

In other words, we need people to get through this life—especially if we want to live it remarkably. Jesus's life on earth shows us how relationships can make a purpose possible.

Finding Your Intimate Few

As an adult, Christ walked through towns and countrysides toward the fulfillment of a great plan—but he rarely walked alone. He carefully chose an inner circle of twelve disciples and friends. He was even more selective when deciding who he drew into his greatest confidences. I call them his intimate few.

Though their efforts were sometimes flawed, his intimate few were relentlessly loyal, and whether they realized it, they were an essential part of Christ's own abundant purpose. Through their journeys together, he poured into them, and they in turn poured into others. The impact of their relationships with Jesus still affects millions of people today, including us.

It is possible that part of your purpose comes from what you pour into the people closest to you. Who are your intimate few?

- Who has your back no matter what?
- Who can you trust with any secret?
- Who can you talk to about your innermost dreams and desires?
- Who will support you in taking steps to do what you were made to do?

As another aspect of fulfilling your purpose, let's turn those questions around.

- Whose back do you have no matter what?
- Whose trust in you is secure, allowing them to share any of their secrets?
- Whose innermost dreams and desires do you listen to?
- Whose steps are you supporting so they can do what they were made to do?

Living an abundant life means not making it all about ourselves. We were created for alliances, connections, and ties with other people, partnerships benefiting both sides. We get what we give. We succeed when we serve. We expand our influence through relationships with other people.

But relationships don't happen without effort. Staying holed up in our houses is not living the amazing life Christ promised. We were made to get out and interact with people who bolster our confidence and help us endure when we're wearing down. Sometimes family believes in us more than we believe in ourselves. And exploring the unknown is usually more fun with friends. In some cases, the converse is true: friends provide the believing, and family brings the fun. When we are pursuing God's will for our lives, Jesus always cheers us on.

If you don't currently have supportive people in your life, there are ways to meet new individuals who will champion your dreams. The key is learning where to go.

Whatever your passion, odds are you can find a group formed around the subject. Painters, pray-ers, pathologists, and paleontologists all congregate. Bakers, beekeepers, bodybuilders, and bus drivers gather. Through my work as a certified personality trainer and leadership facilitator, I know that coroners, law enforcement officers, firefighters, 911 dispatchers, paramedics, and other EMS workers lean on one another. As a business coach, I attend events where bankers, hospital workers, and recreation owners meet. As a writer, I connect with other wordsmiths.

When we assemble and network together, the benefits follow us after we go home. Once everyone parts ways, we can enjoy additional advantages. And sometimes the value increases, when one connection leads to another and deeper relationships develop.

Forming Triple-Cord Relationships

When I attended my first writer's conference, I went alone. The only person I knew was a woman named Kathryn Graves, and we'd only met briefly at another course we'd attended in Texas. But it was enough for her to take me under her wing.

She introduced me to several authors and a few instructors, one named Karen Jordan. Something sparked between Kathryn, Karen, and me. The three of us experienced a rare and immediate bond. We became instant lifetime friends; it didn't matter that we lived in different states.

No matter what your dream or call, relational connections can provide the support necessary to keep you motivated and moving forward. As in my case, sometimes they happen without effort, but more commonly you need to seek and cultivate bonds with people who share similar interests. When there are people in your life who get you, they can provide the encouragement and energy you need when you begin to feel discouraged or depleted. Such moments happen to all of us.

Through our writing journeys, Karen, Kathryn, and I have lived out Ecclesiastes 4:9–12: "Two are better than one because they have a good return for their labor. For if either of them falls, the one will lift up his companion. But woe to the one who falls when there is not another to lift him up. Furthermore, if two lie down together they keep warm, but how can one be warm alone? And if one can overpower him who is alone, two can resist him. A cord of three strands is not quickly torn apart" (NASB).

Our triple-cord relationship is based not only on personal interest but also on professionalism, something we have all needed. Each of us has weathered, and will yet weather, rough winds while navigating the writing world. Illness, accidents, computer issues, and even death won't wait for writers to pen articles or authors to finish their books.

Karen, Kathryn, and I have all needed encouragement to pick up the computer again. We share the belief that every experience holds potential writing fodder. We three amigas have called many times to vent and laugh.

The intimate few inside my author's circle get me, because they understand my passion. I discovered this priceless support system by attending conferences. And every industry, vocation, hobby, profession, endeavor, or interest offers similar ways to connect with like-minded individuals.

An exceedingly abundant life is not spent alone. Connect with others who share your interests. Join associations, organizations, and groups. Attend conferences, seminars, and one-day trainings. If you can't afford to go in person—which I highly recommend over digital platforms—then become part of an online forum until you can save up.

A Pure Purpose

As you chase God's call and your dreams, I have only one caution: whatever you do, don't replace your loved ones with a new obsession.

No matter what you accomplish, if there is no one to share your achievements with, loneliness waits for you at the top. I've met many wealthy, high-positioned, successful women and men whose personal relationships were a train wreck. Resolve not to let this happen to you.

Healthy bonds don't happen by accident. They are the result of intrinsic callings. Instead of complaining about the things your spouse, child, parent, sibling, other family members, friends, or coworkers aren't doing, ask yourself what it is *you're* investing in the relationship. *Really* investing. What are you doing to make things better versus blaming others for your bitterness? As much as they are willing, involve your family and friends in your life—all aspects of it.

When you think about your relationships, consider this important caution. Throughout the Bible, you will see that God's plan never includes destroying families. Make sure your professional connections are appropriate and pure. Don't let your desires become lusts; don't allow temptation to steal your ultimate joy. This is not what you were made for.

I've seen too many fall when their personal pursuit became a priority it was never intended to be. Part of your purpose is to protect the people God placed in your life, not hurt them. Make sure the relationships you are cozying up to are honoring to God.

Wherever you find yourself, ask God to place safe people in your life who will help you accomplish what he desires. And ask him to deposit you in the lives of those you can support as they search for deeper meaning. Remember, it's not all about you or me, and it's not only about now. As we'll discover in the next chapter, a crucial success strategy is learning how to overcome procrastination.

MIND, BODY, AND SPIRIT STRENGTHENERS

YOUR ABUNDANT PURPOSE CHALLENGE

If you don't already have a solid group of people supporting you, set a goal to join one new group within the next thirty days. Become a member of an association or organization.

Sign up for a conference or one-day training session. Look for anything that puts you in contact with others who share interests similar to yours—preferably in person. And don't forget to check yourself. How are you treating your loved ones as you pursue your passion?

YOUR ABUNDANT PURPOSE EXERCISE

Give as well as take. Pour into your intimate few. What matters to them? What have they always wanted to do? Two heads dream bigger than one.

YOUR ABUNDANT PURPOSE SCRIPTURE

Hebrews 10:24–25: "Let us think of ways to motivate one another to acts of love and good works. And let us not neglect our meeting together, as some people do, but encourage one another, especially now that the day of his return is drawing near."

YOUR ABUNDANT PURPOSE PROMISE

You are not alone—God has written similar interests onto the hearts of others. Part of abundant living is seeking until you find those appropriate people.

YOUR ABUNDANT PURPOSE STUDY AND DISCUSSION PROMPTS

Is there anyone you would trust your secret dreams with? Have you told them? Why or why not? If not, where could you go to find trusted people who understand your God-given desires?

Have you become intentional about surrounding yourself with healthy, supportive people? If not, who could become part of your intimate few? Have you asked God to reveal them or to bring them across your path?

Who are you pouring into? Who are you encouraging, supporting, and inspiring to live out their God-size dreams? How are you investing in your loved ones?

CHAPTER 7

Made for Productivity

Labor is the great source from which nearly all, if not all, human comforts and necessities are drawn.

—Abraham Lincoln, "Speech at Cincinnati, Ohio," September 17, 1859

Procrastination undermines our efforts to unearth our purpose. If we aren't productive as God defines it, we cannot fulfill his plans. There are times we are told to do no more than sit at his feet, be still, listen, and learn, and there are times we need to get up and move. The key is to follow God's lead in fulfilling your purpose.

Any person who sets out on a mission, follows a quest, or has their eye on a prize will fight him- or herself at some point. The allure of procrastination has a mighty pull, but not just for the things we dislike. Delays also drag down our dreams.

Every person I've met, from painters to teachers, business owners to stay-at-home parents, and doctors to singers, battles the urge to put important things off. Many of my author friends and I commiserate, "Why does scrubbing the toilet become so inviting when I need to meet a writing deadline?"

Whether we are struggling to put our bodies in motion or fighting the impulse to overdo, we are all susceptible. Procrastination may be behind the reason you haven't figured out what your abundant purpose is. Odds are, your soul senses what you were made for, but you've buried it so deeply, you've forgotten. Once you felt confident in your abilities. You dared to dream big, compliments encouraged you, and you knew you were made for something special. Then life happened. You were likely young when you shut down.

Distractions pulled you away. You felt guilty for allowing yourself to consider it. Other people listed all the reasons you shouldn't go there. You hadn't yet put all the pieces of the puzzle together when some major event turned your life upside down, scattering your hopes, ideas, and aspirations. It's happened to many of us.

Unearthing Dreams

I was a young teen. An early summer breeze swayed the tree branch I sat on, blowing my auburn hair into my eyes, stirring the honeysuckle scents below me. I had a tomboy tendency, so I climbed a lot. I liked gaining new perspectives from the view at the top.

Up in trees and at the local fire tower, I felt free—free to explore, ponder, and dream. At lofty positions, nothing hindered my thoughts or inhibited my creativity. I imagined what my future might look like as various scenarios played in my mind. I sensed whispers of promise coming from a still, small voice. I didn't know it then, but that voice belonged to God.

On this particular day, I would climb for one of the last times. A storm brewed on the horizon, the first of many.

Dad was a mine worker, and there were talks of a strike. People in our community were feuding; threats were escalating. I overheard the conversations my parents had as they weighed their concerns over crossing or not crossing a potential picket line.

"If I cross the line, there's no telling what some of the men will do," Dad said. "But if I don't cross, how will we eat or pay the bills?"

I ran outside. My fantasies about the future seemed silly in comparison to the weight of those current events. I heaped the first pile of emotional dirt onto my dreams.

We eventually uprooted and moved out of state, leaving everything and everyone I'd known behind. The next few years passed in a fog.

I had my first child at seventeen. My parents divorced. I graduated from high school and got married. (Yes, in that order.) And I went to work.

As days turned into years and more "adulting" was required, I became adept at hunkering down, burying my feelings, and distracting myself with activity, anything to get by. For a time, I gave up on God. I didn't notice I'd stopped climbing.

I started hearing the whispers again when I stopped running from God. As I prayed and read the Bible, old memories and longings began to bubble up. I felt a gnawing and knowing that my Maker had made me for incredibly more than I'd allowed myself to experience. At first, I wallowed in self-pity over lost time, bad decisions, and dead dreams. I had a lack mentality. But God didn't give up on me. He continued to speak.

He told me my dreams weren't dead; they simply needed unearthing. I'd left them dormant and needed to dig them up by giving myself permission to remember. I started to pray, asking the Holy Spirit to remind me of what I'd buried.

I remember reading Joel 2:25 and realizing that God was speaking directly to me: "I will restore to you the years that the swarming locust has eaten" (NKJV). I had no idea what, how, where, or when, but God was promising to resurrect my dreams. If I did not get in his way, he would restore my life in spite of any past decision or uncontrollable circumstance.

I came to understand that even time was not a hindrance to God. I was not too old to accomplish his will. God can stop time and start time (Josh. 10:13; Gen. 1:5). The Creator of time will generate all we need if we'll ask.

Ultimately, God showed me other aspects of my purpose when I was ready. But first I had to prove myself. If he couldn't trust me with step one, he would never lead me to step two and beyond (Luke 16:10).

Maybe this hits a place in your own soul.

You've got a clear vision of your purpose but find yourself procrastinating, even though you want to fulfill it with all your heart. If so, resolve to take one step forward within the next twenty-four hours. God is willing to provide the determination, discipline, and endurance you need to succeed when you ask.

Living Out Your Abundant Purpose

The biggest secret, and the first step to discovering, unearthing, and succeeding at your purpose, is to partner your desires with God's. Your Maker crafted you for something very specific. No matter what it is, pour your best into it. Can you say without pause that you are exerting excellence into rooting out all opportunities?

What is God saying to you? Even if it's been years since you consulted him specifically about your dreams, your purpose, and his plans, it's not too late to listen for his still, small voice. He will restore the years the locusts have eaten.

Or perhaps you're entering a new phase in your life, a new element of God's purpose for you. Is he nudging you out of your comfortable existence? What is he whispering into your spirit as you read this book?

What comes to you so naturally that you think it's no big deal? What do other people consistently compliment you for? What's gnawing at you to do? What makes your heart palpitate? It's often more a matter of acting on God's will than not truly knowing it. Sometimes it's more comfortable to be like everyone else instead of daring to be the person God made you to be. Accept yourself while simultaneously investing all available energy, time, money, and other resources into seeking and living out your high calling.

Decision is the second step—and to take that step, you must decide to move in spite of how you feel. You can usually find fear at the heart of procrastination, so don't forget to take courage, no matter where you are in fulfilling your purpose. With God's support and your determination, you can become one of the 1 percent who actually *do* something about their hopes instead of just thinking, dreaming, and talking about them.

I am confident you were made for something that not only stirs you out of bed in the morning but allows you to pour into other people. The third step to living an abundant life is to identify and accept your unique wiring. When you discover your passion for productive endeavors and experience the satisfaction of a job well done, you will begin to reap the joy of your very existence. But not all callings look alike.

Killing Feelings of Insignificance

Underplaying the importance of your giftings can lead to procrastination. If you don't see how you contribute, you might stop putting effort into what you are made to do. The quiet petition of prayer-closet warriors is as important as the message delivered from a spotlighted stage. The mommy who fixes her daughter's breakfast matters as much as the neurosurgeon who fixes a brain. The friend who offers a listening ear and compassionate heart makes as much of a difference as a psychologist listening to patients in her office. If you're wired for the spotlight, embrace your gifting. But conversely, don't despise what may look small in the eyes of the world. Offering a smile and a warm welcome can change someone else's whole day—or life. Kelsi is one of those people for me.

I look forward to interacting with Kelsi, a fast-food employee I see infrequently. Imagining her warm tone and friendly attitude is often enough to propel me to the drive-through for a bottle of water and light snack when I would otherwise pass.

When Kelsi works, I can count on the cheerful tone in her distinctive voice, and her welcoming demeanor. She's professional, productive, and pleasant, and she makes a difference every time I interact with her. By the faces of other customers I've seen, I'd say I'm not the only one she impacts positively. It's hard to remain in a foul mood when you're in Kelsi's presence; even thinking of her improves my outlook.

Kelsi is an example I want to follow. She reminds me that it isn't just what we do but how we go about our day that makes a difference. I can see great purpose in how this woman completes her job. But just imagine if Kelsi began to believe the lie that her fast-food job made her less-than. What if she developed a defeated attitude and stopped passing out joy?

If you have a Kelsi in your life, make it your personal mission to tell them every chance you get, "Thank you for making my day better." Let's encourage people like Kelsi to keep investing their talents, because we all benefit when they do. Encouragers need encouragement too. When we cheer others on, we energize their spirits and lift our own, helping kill the enemy of productivity. Procrastination withers when appreciation is nurtured—even if few know.

Unsung heroes surround us. People who live out their full potential by fulfilling ordinary roles in extraordinary ways. Women and men whose conduct we would do well to imitate.

No matter what we do, we have a chance to make a meaningful difference and fulfill a purpose beyond ourselves when we work as if working unto the Lord (Col. 3:23). That's true no matter what position we hold or whether anyone besides God recognizes it.

I often think about the unnamed people who supported the greats in the Bible and contributed to their big accomplishments. For instance, who were the untold faces and families who served Abraham, the men and women who made his journey of faith possible? What about the laborers whose sharp minds, specialized skills, and strong backs helped rebuild Nehemiah's wall? Or the servants who poured the water Jesus turned into wine as his first miracle? And what of those who assisted a blind Saul of Tarsus before God changed his name to Paul?

Every unnamed person who supported God's work in the Bible holds a unique place in history. Without their productive efforts, we would not have the motivating history we lean on today.

These unnamed supporters did not let a lack mentality hinder their productivity. Lack of recognition, title, or high position did not keep them from producing marvelous things for God's kingdom and helping their fellow man. They weren't designated for a spotlight, but they made a quiet yet powerful impact.

We too often forget that success is not determined solely by what we do but also by how well we do it and the attitude with which we undertake it. Whether your gift comes from offering simple smiles to complete strangers or from mastering the complexities of an algebraic mystery, using your talents is what matters most. A buried talent is a dead talent. Whether anyone else sees or not, we must act to make an impact.

Conquering Rationalization

If you want to discover and unearth your abundant purpose, do not rationalize. One thing you can count on when procrastination kicks in: it induces rationalization. Don't blame anyone else; don't wait for someone else to motivate you. Get up and do something when you can, while you can.

A common series of justifications leads to excuses and inaction:

- I'm too exhausted.
- I don't have enough time.
- I don't have the energy.
- I don't have the money.
- I'm not in the mood.
- I need to do something for someone else.
- I'll do it tomorrow.

But self-talk works positively as well as negatively. You can talk yourself up as well as down:

- I'm wide awake and alert.
- I don't know what may happen in the next twenty-four hours, so I need to make the best use of this time while I have it.
- I am vibrant, strong, and enthusiastic.
- I need to work enough to live but not so much that I'm living to work.
- I will protect the time, space, and other resources I need to pursue my purpose.

- I must get up every day and refuse to let myself off the hook until I've accomplished my goals for the day.
- This cannot wait until tomorrow; I'll do it right now.

Do not allow yourself to get away with saying, "I'll just sit down for one minute," or, "I'll just watch one TV show." One leads to more and more until time slips away. Instead, use short increments of time in your favor.

The smallest amount of motion can lead to a great deal of momentum. Start with a little movement. Say, "I'll walk, write, clean, paint, practice, research, work on my project [or whatever it is you are putting off] for five minutes." And see where it leads you. Discipline is oddly freeing. It does not hold us in bondage, as we often fear. In reality, as God tells us, "Work brings profit, but mere talk leads to poverty" (Prov. 14:23). And there is no greater prosperity than the fulfillment of your God-given purpose.

Keeping Promises

If you want to experience an abundant life, kick procrastination to the wayside. Paraphrasing Ecclesiastes 5:5, I often remind myself it's better not to make a promise than to make one and break it. I would offer the same counsel to you: don't break promises—even those to yourself.

Exhibit integrity at an intrinsic level, doing the same thing whether or not you believe anyone else can see or hear you. God is looking for those who keep their commitments. If you have said you will take action, then do it. If you have stated your intent to sit still, listening for God's direction, then keep your word. Either way, your productive efforts will be rewarded.

Procrastination *is* poison, but productivity is a restorative potion. Forward movement is part of God's plan for our lives, especially helpful when we stand out from those in the crowd. We'll delve into your unique role next.

MIND, BODY, AND SPIRIT STRENGTHENERS

YOUR ABUNDANT PURPOSE CHALLENGE

Review times in your past when you succeeded. What can you duplicate? What do you absolutely know that works? Consider each step that took you where you wanted to go, and make a list of the details that could help you accomplish what you want today.

YOUR ABUNDANT PURPOSE EXERCISE

Create a Purpose Plan. Schedule your next best step with a date and time deadline. Decide who and what needs to be involved. Where do you need to go next? In your written plan, include a Why statement: Why is this pursuit important to you? Black-and-white outlines tell our brains we are serious.

YOUR ABUNDANT PURPOSE SCRIPTURE

Galatians 6:9 (NIV): "Let us not become weary in doing good, for at the proper time we will reap a harvest if we do not give up."

YOUR ABUNDANT PURPOSE PROMISE

Tiny action steps lead to great destinations.

YOUR ABUNDANT PURPOSE STUDY AND DISCUSSION PROMPTS

What might you gain by taking immediate action in pursuit of your purpose right now? What might you risk if you wait?

How can you break up your projects, goals, and aspirations into bite-size time pieces? What can you do for five minutes to get you started?

What are the vital things you must do in order to achieve your goals and fulfill your purpose? What are feasible and manageable stages that are crucial to your success?

CHAPTER 8
Made for Acceptance

Wisdom . . . is knowing what you have to accept.

—Wallace Stegner, *Angle of Repose*

Facts don't change, but perspective can. As a certified personality trainer, I often teach people about the different ways human beings can view the world around them. Two people can look at the exact same image but see two very different things—or at the very least, focus on opposing details.

For instance, one of my favorite icebreakers when facilitating a meeting with people I am getting to know is to share an image around the room. I ask attendees to quickly view the picture, keep what they see to themselves, and then pass the illustration on. After everyone has had the opportunity to view it, one by one, I ask each person to tell us what they saw. Often, perplexed looks are exchanged as one person describes one thing while another reports something very different. I find the time is well spent to help each individual finally see both images hidden in the picture.

These are called ambiguous images, and you can google the term to find many online examples. They prove that not everything is clear at first glance.

Like the ambiguous images I use for demonstration, God uses each of us individually, though we are part of a larger whole. And just as we want others to allow us to be who God created us to be, we should offer the same consideration to our fellow human beings.

Agreeing to Disagree

Part of loving our neighbors is accepting them for who they are and the different ways they view the world. Disagreement is not an issue as long as we agree to disagree respectfully, in a God-honoring way. We were made to contribute diversely, not divisively.

But in today's pressure-filled society, too often even those who love Jesus conform or get sucked into a vortex of disrespectful debates. "Right-fighting"—pushing, shoving, and jockeying to be seen as right while proving others wrong—has become an online sport. Participating in public brawls is a good way to undermine your purpose, no matter what your skills or mission.

I'll call her Christy, professional photographer and right-fighter extraordinaire. A benign Facebook post about a political hot topic triggered her and unleashed a side of Christy never seen before.

She could have kept her comments to herself; after all, the original post was not derogatory or offensive. But it reflected a view that opposed Christy's own. So she took her aggressive comments public, and the verbal pileup began.

Name-calling, belief bashing, profanity popping, and Jesus lovers pitted against Jesus lovers caused the social media site to blow up for days. When the dust settled, nothing was resolved. Rather, several relationships were decimated. Most people dug more deeply into their convictions and stood stubbornly on their stances. No minds were changed, some former friends became enemies, and businesses lost clients—Christy's business included.

The social media callouts, finger-pointing, nitpicking, and superior-intelligence attitudes had taken their toll. After the shake-up finally died down, the most painful consequence for Christy came in the form of aftershocks when texts, phone calls, and emails no longer were returned. Most people wouldn't talk to her at all, but a couple of her former clients spoke up bluntly and cut Christy's soul with a spiritual knife.

A local contractor said, "I'm sorry, I just can't do business with you anymore. I thought you were a Christian, but I saw what you posted on Facebook and I don't want to get mixed up in that kind of drama."

At first, Christy felt defensive, thinking she was being blackballed for her political beliefs. She tried to make her point. "I don't think it's fair that you're judging me this way. I have a right to my opinions just like everyone else does, and I was simply expressing my views."

"I'm not condemning you. You are certainly entitled to your ideals," the man said. "And frankly, you and I probably agree on many points. But it's as much *how* we say something as *what* we say that can cause destruction."

Christy felt heat rise up her neck and her voice rose with it. "So I'm supposed to be a doormat for other people to walk on? They can treat me however they want, and I'm supposed to lie down and take it?"

He sighed. "You are a gifted young woman with a lot of potential, but I learned a long time ago that if you want to succeed in any business, you must learn to tame your tongue. Getting along with people is the most important skill you will possess. Working peacefully will help you survive. To paraphrase Paul from 1 Corinthians 6:12, 'All things are permissible, but not all things are beneficial.'"

Christy shifted uncomfortably as she began to mentally review all the reasons her online comments were justified.

The man looked Christy firmly in the eye, but his tone was compassionate and gentle. "Human nature makes us less likely to listen to someone who pushes their opinions, beliefs, or thoughts at us. Consider God's example. He doesn't force himself on us; he listens and loves, and his forgiveness and acceptance are what draw us to him."

Christy opened her mouth but closed it before she said something she would regret.

After several seconds, the man filled the silence. "Look, I'm simply saying that if we want others to listen to us, we would do well to listen to them first. Arguments and heated debates get us nowhere, especially in a public forum. People might like to watch the action, but few want to be around a person who's ripped someone else to shreds. None of us wants to be next."

Christy could remain silent no longer. "I hear you, but I don't feel like I did anything wrong. I still say I have the right to tell others what I think."

A look of resignation covered the man's features. "I also have the right to take my business elsewhere. Peace and professionalism are qualities I expect in my affiliations. So I wish you well and will pray for you." Then he turned and walked away.

Christy's anger toward the man grew with each step he took. But after a few days of replaying their conversation, and an encounter with another client at the post office, she began to think twice about her reaction.

Sarah was one of Christy's first customers. Christy liked and respected the fortysomething Realtor. Sarah was sharp and forthright but also kind—plus, her listings helped keep Christy in business. But as they came eye to eye by the outgoing-mail slot, Christy knew something was off.

"Hey, Sarah. I've been trying to reach you. I guess you've been super busy. I've got some ideas about adding a few creative elements to your marketing pieces. I think it will help gain more interest in your properties. I'd love to share them with you as soon as you have time."

An odd look shadowed Sarah's face. "I have been busy, but mostly, I've been trying to figure out what to say to you."

"Oh?" Christy felt a prickle of concern blossom up her spine.

"I saw the shots fired in the Facebook war you were involved in. It was even conversation at this month's Chamber of Commerce meeting."

Christy felt queasy. "I realize it might have looked bad, and I probably shouldn't have gone public that way, but I get tired of feeling like I don't have a voice."

The woman placed a sympathetic hand on Christy's shoulder. "There's nothing wrong with voicing your thoughts, but there is a respectful and professional way to go about it. It disappointed me to see that you initiated the debate, and I was even more disheartened at your unwillingness to hear other people. I believe in you and your work. God has given you a beautiful gift, and I want to see you succeed, but a defensive attitude turns people off."

Christy felt stung by Sarah's expression of disappointment and considered a rebuttal. But she willed her mouth to remain shut and listened instead.

Sarah offered an encouraging smile. "I'll give you another chance, but only if you assure me that you will not participate in that kind of exchange again. Some of my clients were involved in that thread, and I cannot afford to have my reputation damaged. I mean it, Christy. You are talented, but I urge you to consider a heart check. I know you are a woman of faith—but did you honor God with your words? Do you think he created you for that purpose? Ability only gets you as far as your attitude takes you. Please understand my motive for saying this: I care about you."

Christy knew Sarah cared. And the similarity between her comments and that of Christy's former male client were not lost on her. She had some soul-searching to do.

It took over a year for Christy to regain the business she lost. In that time, she read and reread Matthew 7:3–5. "Why worry about a speck in your friend's eye when you have a log in your own? How can you think of saying to your friend, 'Let me help you get rid of that speck in your eye,' when you can't see past the log in your own eye? Hypocrite! First get rid of the log in your own eye; then you will see well enough to deal with the speck in your friend's eye."

Her open heart, transparency, humility, and vulnerability paid off. She had learned a priceless lesson. Yes, God had given her a talent for photography, but Christy now knew that how she used her gift would determine her effectiveness as a photographer. She posted Philippians 4:5 on her bathroom mirror: "Let your gentleness be evident to all. The Lord is near" (NIV). Christy's mistake and her willingness to learn from it are something that can educate all of us.

Can't you tell when a person is overly defensive, bitter, angry, or jealous? Doesn't it taint your outlook when someone persistently points out flaws in other people and processes? No one is looking for a chronic complainer or corrector. After all, who are any of us to play God's role? Our purpose is not to fix others or right-fight our way to victory.

I've learned I don't know half as much as I often think I do, and other people often know more than I initially give them credit for. I could spend all day telling you about my errors and the consequences I've reaped from trying to correct others and how those attempts backfired. I impaired my ability to influence people and fulfill my true purpose when I focused on being right.

Though I'll never achieve perfection in this area, incorporating strategic Scripture verses into my life has transformed my effectiveness. I've watched God increase my influence and do exceedingly abundantly more in my life than I ever could have dreamed.

Battling the Need to Be Right

Most right-fighting stems from insecurity. We fear someone else is going to get something we desire, usually tied to our sense of inner value. We covet their possessions or popularity, their special giftings or strengths, or the way life seems to treat them in comparison to what happens to us. We might deny the matter, telling ourselves we don't want anything they have, but our actions speak truths we won't confess, even to ourselves.

Ultimately, fighting to prove our worth only makes us less attractive and effective. Instead, "fix your thoughts on what is true, and honorable, and right, and pure, and lovely, and admirable. Think about things that are excellent and worthy of praise" (Phil. 4:8). Applying this passage to thoughts and actions daily will change your life.

I'm not telling you not to have strong views. Don't cower or conform, and don't let others walk on your beliefs or make you feel ashamed of Jesus. Just be mindful of his example:

- Turn the other cheek (Matt. 5:39).
- Pray for those who spitefully use you (Luke 6:28).

- If someone is attacking or wrongfully accusing you, remember, "the Lord himself will fight for you. Just stay calm" (Exod. 14:14).

Instinct might tell you to avoid social media, and if you simply cannot control your outbursts, that may be the best choice. However, what if you could fulfill an exceedingly exceptional purpose by setting a positive example online? What if you are the one God is calling to spread a unique and lasting light in an otherwise dark world?

- What if you listened more and voiced personal opinions less?
- What if you could inspire, motivate, and encourage others who feel stuck or depressed?
- What if your gentle answers defused anger in people (Prov. 15:1)?
- What if God used you to demonstrate Christ's loving-kindness, mercy, and forgiveness to others?

Remember, God fashioned you as an individual. There is something wonderfully *you* about the way he wired you. God wants to use you to deliver blessings to others in ways that are unique to you. Discover and develop your own abilities, then use them to bring good and not harm. Consider the following:

- How might God use your baking skills to offer a symbol of your remorse for hurting someone?
- When might your way with words encourage another person, especially someone who is feeling defeated, attacked, or worthless?
- Who could use the bright colors you paint to brighten their drab existence?
- Where could you sing to spread joy and hope?
- What can your powerful prayers do to strengthen the weak or lost?
- Why not offer a listening ear? Few experience this special gift that makes people feel accepted, esteemed, and cared for.

I cannot imagine a more important purpose than honoring God in word and deed. Accept yourself. Dare to be different from the rest of the world by sharing truth in gentle ways. Accept others. Respect diverse thoughts, even when you humbly but boldly agree to disagree.

Human beings are not created in cookie-cutter fashion. What a boring existence that would be! And our God is anything but boring. What kind of personality do you have? What background and experience has taught you lessons you can share in a loving way? How can you offset the negativity in the world around you? What can you give that no one else is offering?

And consider: Whose natural giftings are *opposite* yours, making that person an ideal partner, bringing balance, and allowing each of you to get more done? How can you bring that person alongside you, benefiting you both? Are the things that grate against you opportunities in disguise? Is this iron sharpening iron (Prov. 27:17)? Do you need to change yourself instead of wishing, praying, or trying to change another? What true, honorable, or admirable traits have you overlooked in someone who drives you crazy?

How does Jesus see the person who frustrates you?

You will hear me say this more than once: make a difference where you can, while you can. Let others be who they are while you excel in all God created you for. And make sure all of your efforts are shrouded in love. This is what you were made to do.

If you feel discomfort where you are or in what you are doing, take time for a soul and heart check. Maybe you need to rethink your attitudes. Perhaps you should make amends. Or maybe God is nudging you to do something unique about the troubles you see—in a way that demonstrates love for others and honor to him.

Whatever the purpose God has placed on your life, when you accept and act on it, you will soon discover even more is waiting for you. An essential aspect of any call is to look out for the interests of others (Phil. 2:4).

MIND, BODY, AND SPIRIT STRENGTHENERS

YOUR ABUNDANT PURPOSE CHALLENGE

Resolve to stand out as the positive voice in the crowd, especially when surrounded by negativity. At work, online, in gatherings of family or friends, ask yourself often, *How does Jesus see these people, and how can I show them his love?*

YOUR ABUNDANT PURPOSE EXERCISE

Review your social media pages and evaluate what you're portraying. Are you loving your neighbor through your posts, or is this an area you could improve on? Make a fresh start with positive post perspectives today.

YOUR ABUNDANT PURPOSE SCRIPTURE

Philippians 2:14–15 (NIV): "Do everything without grumbling or arguing, so that you may become blameless and pure, 'children of God without fault in a warped and crooked generation.' Then you will shine among them like stars in the sky."

YOUR ABUNDANT PURPOSE PROMISE

The differences between you and others are divinely designed, so you can make a difference no one else can, and others can too.

YOUR ABUNDANT PURPOSE STUDY AND DISCUSSION PROMPTS

What are some of the harder personalities for you to deal with? What are some of the easier personalities for you to get along with? How can the ones you struggle with, as well as the ones you naturally tolerate, help you use your gifts for an extraordinary good?

Do you think dissension is increasing or decreasing in the world? Why or why not?

Are there problems, issues, or challenges you see that other people seem blind to? Could your awareness bring about a resolution, improvement, or solution? Is it possible you're the one who sees it because you're the one called to do something about it?

CHAPTER 9

Made for Leadership

The high destiny of the individual is to serve rather than to rule.

—Albert Einstein, "Science and Religion"

Whether you spend most of your waking hours parenting, directing, training, or serving, you are leading. Someone is watching you and mimicking your behavior—a student, your son or daughter, an employee, your spouse. The people around you pick up on your verbiage and gestures, including coworkers, close friends, nieces or nephews, or the athletes you coach. What you say and how you treat people even impacts the salesclerk who waits on you.

Your conduct is being evaluated constantly. At any moment, we are either leading or following—sometimes both, simultaneously. Parents navigate their kids through childhood, but children also guide their parents into maturity. Managers train their employees, but employees also teach their managers. We all lead someone; the question is, Are we leading well?

Purposeful leadership is the foundation of an exceedingly abundant life. It's a role every Christ follower is eventually called to fulfill. Jesus told his disciples to "go and make disciples" (Matt. 28:19).

Once you say yes to Jesus's invitation for a personal relationship, you become his follower or disciple. For most, this is a lifelong commitment, one that includes obeying his command to go and make new disciples. In other words, your ultimate purpose is to share, teach, and lead, after you set the example of following well. It might sound overwhelming and complicated, but you can do this in simple and ordinary ways.

Wing Lifter Versus Wing Clipper

At some point, everyone needs support. Regardless of position or pay grade, we are all people with problems as well as things we would like to celebrate. And because you are a leader, you have the opportunity to influence well. Will you be a wing clipper or a wing lifter?

I've been both. Lifters shoo people out of their comfortable nests, encourage, build up, see things in another person that the person may not see in themselves. They ask questions and show genuine interest in the other person. They listen twice as much as they speak, draw good things out, and guide wisely instead of squelching potential by trying to control and fix.

Lifters celebrate when the people around them succeed—they don't see someone else's victory as something to destroy. By investing their interest in others, they themselves benefit. I like what Zig Ziglar said: "You can have everything in life you want if you will just help enough other people get what they want."[1] This is leading well.

Wing clippers, on the other hand, take credit even when it isn't due. They are territorial, possessive, narcissistic, and live in fear and insecurity that someone else might succeed or look better than they do. They fight to be right and battle to be heard. They overtalk, undercut, and overshadow. Clippers find reasons to criticize rather than compliment. When pressure hits, their influencing traits are not admirable—anger, frustration, negativity, and put-downs abound. If they do pretend to care, their true concerns are for themselves.

Clippers also restrain themselves inappropriately. When given the chance to do something meaningful for another, they usually let someone else take the risk *and* the reward. We were not made to diminish our own blessings, as clippers usually do.

You were created to be a wing lifter. Leading by lifting is part of your call; you're created to help other people fly. Part of your purpose includes setting a consistent (not perfect) example for others to follow—but maybe not in the way you would assume.

Effective Leadership

In its purest form, leading means serving people and meeting them at their greatest needs. To become an exceptional leader, something to which we all should aspire, we must authentically care more for others than for ourselves (1 Cor. 10:24).

Christ was the most effective leader who ever walked the face of this planet because of his commitment to serve others sacrificially. Christ was merciful and kind while equally strong and powerful. He showed us how to live wise as a serpent and gentle as a dove. Depending on what the situation called for, he was either tender or firm. He was as intentional about following the design for his life as he was committed to taking command of the assignment God called him to.

Still today, Jesus Christ is the king of compassion—because he knows from experience that great leaders learn most from their greatest hardships:

- How could he understand our sorrows had he not known his own?
- How could he take us anywhere if he wasn't familiar with the terrain himself?
- How could he speak authentically if his past wasn't relevant?
- How could he show us how to rise above had he not been buried himself?

Most of us want to start at the top. We wish to avoid the pain, sweat, and anguish of working our way from the bottom up; instead, we hope to fast-track so we can get there sooner. But these desires are a detriment.

To lead well, we need to work our way through processes, learning why important steps are there and what they are. We learn from adversity; it strengthens our mental and emotional muscles, making us stronger and more flexible.

Slowing down actually takes us further faster, reducing stumbles and wrong turns. Like Christ, strong leaders accept a season of weakening as part of their growth; they consider it resistance training for the spirit.

Strength in the Thin Places

You can't help shape others if you haven't been worked over yourself. I find it fascinating how many times the Bible references people as lumps of clay. There's more to a lump of clay than first meets the eye. Let's consider why, starting with a few Bible verses:

> How foolish can you be? He is the Potter, and he is certainly greater than you, the clay! Should the created thing say of the one who made it, "He didn't make me"? Does a jar ever say, "The potter who made me is stupid"? (Isa. 29:16)

> And yet, O Lord, you are our Father. We are the clay, and you are the potter. We all are formed by your hand. (Isa. 64:8)

> The Lord gave another message to Jeremiah. He said, "Go down to the potter's shop, and I will speak to you there." So I did as he told me and found the potter working at his wheel. But the jar he was making did not turn out as he had hoped, so he crushed it into a lump of clay again and started over. (Jer. 18:1–4)

At first, these Scripture verses might not appear to have anything to do with leadership, and on the surface they certainly don't sound appealing. But when you look deeper and consider what a potter does with clay, how his handling of it changes the outcome and shapes its purpose, clay begins to look much more attractive.

A friend first made me aware of the pottery-making process. We were discussing some difficulties I was going through at the time, and weighing the various reasons God might allow them to happen. She taught me something I've never forgotten. The relevance of her story has proven itself time and again as I faced other tough periods, enabling me to pass those lessons on to others.

We were sitting in my car at the local park, barely paying attention to the exercisers walking in circles. Cara turned to face me. "Your situation makes me think of the Scripture passage that says God is the potter and we are the clay. Have you ever made pottery?"

I laughed. "We both know I am not an artist, and I'm certainly not good at putting things together. I'm pretty sure pottery and me would equal disaster."

Cara smiled in amusement. "Well, my teacher taught us how to make pottery in art class. You start out with this soft, pliable piece of clay that's flexible and easy to mold. You shape it the way you want it and let it dry. But if you don't fix the flaws before the clay cures completely, they'll permanently set. Cracks, thin places, or even too much clay in one area weighs the piece down and will cause droops and brittleness that weaken the vessel. If you don't repair those things before the clay hardens, the final product will end up useless. So do you know what you do?"

"Throw it in the trash?"

She chuckled, and her ebony eyes sparkled. "You could. But does God toss us in the trash when we don't turn out exactly the way he wants the first time?"

"I've never considered that."

"Even a partially dried but imperfect piece of pottery is still usable. The potter just has to make some adjustments. They aren't easy on the clay, but the results are worth it in the end. Sometimes you have to punch and pummel, starting from scratch to produce pliable clay again. A potter often needs to scrape away excess in order to fill cracks and gaps. You push and pull to spread the clay evenly. And everything is done with a gentle hand, ensuring you don't break the vessel into bits."

She had my full attention. I thought about the Scripture verses referring to us as clay, and I imagined God's hand shaping us as Cara described.

She continued. "Sometimes you have to put the clay through this process several times until you finally get the smooth shape you want. But you don't want it too perfect. A few flaws add character and uniqueness. Strength, more than an unblemished exterior, is needed in the thin places.

"Once you are satisfied with the structure of the vessel, you apply a glaze and fire it in a kiln. When you remove it, the former lump of clay comes out as a gorgeous piece of art. After a good cleaning, it's ready to share with the world."

Cara's description of pottery creation makes me think of us. When we try to lead without consulting God, we cause cracks, gaps, and thin places in our own lives as well as in those we hope to guide. Sometimes our strengths become weaknesses when we maximize our time and energy in one area while neglecting another. Often we force the Potter to start over. But he doesn't despise us for our flaws. Instead, he allows them to give us character, strength, and deeper beauty. Every handmade person is unique.

James 1:2–4 tells us to "consider it pure joy, my brothers and sisters, whenever you face trials of many kinds, because you know that the testing of your faith produces perseverance. Let perseverance finish its work so that you may be mature and complete, not lacking anything" (NIV). During my own challenging periods, God was preparing me for leadership, teaching me perseverance so I could stand mature and complete—still imperfect, but fully equipped. How could I lead well if I hadn't been strengthened by difficulty?

Leaders require whittling. Rough edges must be smoothed. Cracks need filling. Thin places benefit from additional support. I found it strangely comforting, when I felt pulverized and beaten down, to know that God was using the process to prepare me for an extraordinary purpose. It also made me think of Jesus.

Not only was Cara's example the perfect analogy for Christ's life, but it reminded me that nothing happened to him by accident. Every detail of his suffering was part of a plan, and the pain he endured strengthened his impact. What Jesus went through made him beautifully relevant to each of us.

We know that Christ understands our suffering because he himself suffered. He gets temptation because he has been tempted. The tiredness we feel is no surprise to him; he too felt exhaustion. But because he persevered and fulfilled God's exceedingly abundant purpose for his life, he knows that we can too. He believes in our ability to endure and overcome.

I have been cured in the oven of adversity many times, but each experience magnified my compassion for others, increased my understanding for what people endure, and enhanced my wisdom for how to help someone else if I could. I believe these are the top three secrets to effective leadership and making a real difference in the world.

Whether I'm guiding one of my children, training church leaders, or coaching the CEO and board members of a multimillion-dollar organization, some of the best teaching materials I possess were derived from times of personal pulverization.

Without experiential empathy, few have a heart to serve and meet people's needs, making it impossible to lead. Leaders who are disconnected from their people dishearten them. But when others know we have a level of care, they are more open to our influence—even in the cutthroat world of business.

When we allow God to bring us to completion, we begin to see a larger plan at work in our lives, something far more exceptional than anything we could have imagined. Whatever place or position we are in, we are made to lead through service and by example. Whether with our spouses, children, extended family members, friends, coworkers, or strangers, each moment is a "such a time as this" chance to make a difference (Esther 4:14).

So let me ask, what are others learning from watching you?

- Do you listen to others as they tell you their needs, or do you predetermine what they want?
- Are you willing to follow as well as to take command?

- Are you praying for opportunities to serve and then looking for people to assist?
- Are you disconnected and disheartening or connected and encouraging?
- Do you see the potential for smoother outcomes from God's whittling work?

These kinds of questions can act as a filter to help you choose wisely and see the events of your life more clearly. When you allow Christ to shape your mind and circumstances, you will begin to understand that godly leadership is part of the amazing life he promised his people. You are made to be a disciple and to create disciples. You are shaped for service. You are called to support and share. There is no satisfaction so great as leading well.

MIND, BODY, AND SPIRIT STRENGTHENERS

YOUR ABUNDANT PURPOSE CHALLENGE

Begin a new mission: look for the purpose in your everyday encounters. Who, what, where, when, how, and why? View every relationship with purposeful eyes. You were created for leadership and influence, so determine to do both well. These basic questions will lead you to influence and help you make the difference you were made for.

YOUR ABUNDANT PURPOSE EXERCISE

Don't think you were made for leadership? Go to a Bible app or website and search the word *lead*. Most biblical translations show over eight hundred references to this term. Leading is an important subject to God. Read his Word and allow him to be your leadership mentor.

YOUR ABUNDANT PURPOSE SCRIPTURE

Proverbs 12:24: "Work hard and become a leader; be lazy and become a slave."

YOUR ABUNDANT PURPOSE PROMISE

You were designed to live and lead well.

YOUR ABUNDANT PURPOSE STUDY AND DISCUSSION PROMPTS

What position(s) has God placed you in "for just such a time as this" (Esther 4:14)?

Are you serving where you can serve or allowing self to make you miss important opportunities?

Are you asking questions and listening closely to others so you can determine true expectations for the purpose of meeting and exceeding them?

CHAPTER 10

Made for Gratitude

Let gratitude be the pillow upon which you kneel to say your nightly prayer.

—Maya Angelou, *Celebrations: Rituals of Peace and Prayer*

What we fill ourselves with splashes onto everyone around us and will either enhance or diminish what we achieve. We were not made for misery. We were made for magnificent joy—but unless we look for it, we will not find it. Read Psalm 136 and you will see that giving thanks is a profound part of the Master's plan for an exceedingly abundant life.

When we intentionally find and express gratitude, our lives take on new clarity and meaning. Our thankful hearts change the way we see the world, making each day richer.

In the introduction of this book, I shared a snippet from my near-death experience following my kidney donation. What I didn't tell you then was how much that terrifying event changed my outlook on life, helping me find and fulfill my purpose. Sometimes losing what we take for granted becomes a catalyst for profound appreciation.

From the surgery, I have a scar on my left side that wraps from front to back, where the surgical team opened me up to remove the kidney. (Today they are able to do this procedure less invasively.) You might think I hate my scar, but in fact I love it fiercely.

For several days following the surgery, my body stung and ached from the cuts made through multiple layers of muscle. The pain worsened when I sneezed or laughed. Sometimes I wanted to punch my husband in the face. He's always made me laugh and took special joy from watching me wince postsurgery. Once, when I moved too fast and pulled my side, I yelped, "It hurts when I breathe." With a twinkle of orneriness in his eye, my husband said, "Well then, stop breathing."

I immediately started laughing harder, then cried as shooting fire stabbed my side.

But my husband was as compassionate as he was playful. Often during those days, he'd rub my arm and say, "Babe, I hope you stop hurting soon."

I did too. It felt as if I'd never be free of pain. But with each passing day my pain level steadily decreased, until one morning I woke up and realized I could move freely without recoiling.

Overcome with gratitude, I practically jumped out of bed, and began to count my many blessings. I could walk to the bathroom like a normal person. I got into the shower unassisted. I was able to bend down and pick up my young son. When I sneezed, I didn't feel inflamed. And my husband's silly jokes no longer made me want to commit bodily harm.

More than twenty years later, I still feel that same level of appreciation because I understand how precious life's little pleasures are. I no longer take normal bodily functions for granted. And when I feel particularly stressed or pressured, I remind myself of one profound truth: if this is the worst thing that happens, it's been a great day!

I can't tell you how many times this has helped me push past worry, fear, or jealousy, all enemies when it comes to fulfilling God's ultimate purpose. Let me show you what I mean:

- *What if I try this and find out it's not really what I'm supposed to do with my life?* If that's the worst thing that happens, then you start over. You can learn lessons, and the experiences will help you grow so you're better prepared for your true high calling in life. This delay is merely a stepping-stone meant to teach and guide.
- *What if I make a fool of myself?* If that's the worst that happens, then you're having a great life. You won't be the first person to do

something embarrassing. Besides, a little humiliation is good for the soul and makes you more relevant and reachable to other people.

- *What if someone else succeeds and I don't, or she succeeds at a higher level than I do?* Celebrate with that person. You are not her and she is not you. There are people you will reach who someone else can't and vice versa. Don't let jealousy over God's gifts to others taint yours. Focus on what you have, not on what you think someone else has more of. That person's successes are God's business. Be happy when others are happy (Rom. 12:15).

In chapter 3 we discussed the impact of practicing presence to increase the happiness in our lives. What we focus on affects how we feel.

Exercising Happiness

Besides practicing presence in the moment, there's an exercise that can boost your happiness level almost instantly, no matter how bad you're feeling. A young mother who reached out to me recently provides a great example for applying this exercise to real-life issues. Her email read:

> I'm about to lose it. I'm exhausted, angry, and beaten to a pulp. No matter what I try, it's not enough. I'm a failure as a wife, mother, and employee. I'm ready to throw my towel in the ring and give up.
>
> I've made myself and my family absolutely miserable. They're not happy, because I'm not happy. I scream and yell, making my kids cry and my husband shut down. I see everyone walking on eggshells, and it makes me sad and mad, all at the same time. The slightest move on their parts can set me off. My blowups usually end with me going to my bedroom, slamming the door, falling on the bed, where I pray and cry, cry and pray. But I think God is tuning me out, like everyone else is.

> Work isn't any better. I can't focus. I'm edgy. I'm missing details. I live on sugar and energy drinks during the day, because I'm too tired to fix anything healthy. I typically eat one meal a day, and most of the time it isn't that nutritious.
>
> I have no willpower. My strength is gone. It's getting harder to keep up the charade. I feel lost and helpless. What am I doing wrong? Why am I such a mess? I know better, so why can't I do better? I need help!

I wish I could say this is the only instance where I've received this kind of message. Sadly, I've heard similar pleas from numerous stay-at-home moms, single career gals, young men fatigued from the fight to keep up, and successful businesspeople who are burned out from the rat race. But the same answer has been of benefit to them all.

When you infuse the simple yet powerful process of intentional gratitude into your daily habits, things change for the better. We were made to be thankful. Here are some suggestions:

1. Give yourself a break and focus on appreciation. What are some gifts, skills, and abilities you are thankful to have? Think on these, and stop listening to the voice that points out every tiny detail you do wrong. From this moment on, refuse to nitpick yourself.
2. Schedule restful meditation. Focus on what God has done for you instead of concentrating on what he's done for others. Take a solo drive in silence, or sneak away for a ten-minute bath—anything that allows you time to think deeply.
3. Allow yourself to live freely, in thankful moderation. Extreme deprivation typically leads to indulgence, even more so than occasional splurges. Praise God for the pleasures he allows as well as the needs he provides. The act of spiritual worship enhances self-discipline.

4. Take note of the small things. The breath you just took. A hug from a child. The shade of your favorite flower. The scent of your preferred hot drink. The sound of birds serenading you from a tree bough. Savor the flavor of your most loved treat. Think of something that made you laugh. Write these things down. Share them with a supportive friend or family member. Express them to God.
5. Do a daily Scripture search for passages that speak of giving thanks and expressing gratitude. We all need something to look forward to, and the power of God's Word in action can cause a monumental mood shift.
6. Ask yourself, "What is one thing I'm taking for granted today that at one time I would have felt grateful for?"
7. Drop the comparison complex. Instead of whining because so-and-so is a great athlete and you're not, thank God for your ability to organize a team. Brandon's presence on the stage does not diminish your skill at quietly moving mountains via God's presence. Tiffany's mastery at crunching numbers has no bearing on your expertise at making others feel heard. Focus on what you've been infused with, and praise God for how he uses you to make a difference.

Giving thanks will increase your sense of hope and belief in yourself. And when you express gratitude for your talents, an odd thing occurs—your awareness of your gifts increases and it opens your eyes to new opportunities for doing something with them.

Training for the Hard Times

When you feel happy and confident inside, you can flourish in your purpose. The weeds of worry, fear, and jealousy have less soil to take root in, so they can't choke you with distraction. Gratitude raises our levels of happiness and confidence, and it's a great motivator.

You can immerse every thought, decision, and action in thanksgiving.

The practice of "small thankfulness" provides training for the moments when gratitude is much harder. It's difficult to give thanks when our kids are sick again, or we're lonely, or overworked, or a deadline is stressing us to the max. But it's a requirement if we want to experience an exceedingly abundant life.

Looking for gratitude in a crisis is beneficial to us. It motivates us to keep moving forward, providing supernatural peace in the midst of chaos. And it's easier when we exercise gratitude regularly. I've done this for years, even with something as silly as expressing thanks for close parking spaces and finding lost keys.

I take Philippians 4:6–7 seriously, where we are told to pray with thanksgiving in all situations. So when I see no sign of a parking spot, I pray like this:

> *Heavenly Father,*
>
> *I thank you that you see my need and are already at work to meet it. I am grateful you care about all the details of my life, large and small. And if it's your will, I praise you in advance for providing a parking space for me today. Thank you, in Jesus's name. Amen.*

You might laugh, or you may think I'm being frivolous with God, but this is serious business to me. When God repeats himself, we need to pay close attention. I've found over one hundred places in the Bible where some form of the word *thanks* is used. And in the rare times he says no, I choose to believe it's for protective measures. Most of the time, I get a great spot for my car.

God desires our gratitude. It's a way for us to express our love, and it releases his power. Just as he can move cars to free up parking spaces, God has no problem aligning our purposes. His power resides in worshipful appreciation. We are made to communicate it.

You can miss some of the reasons for your existence by undervaluing the skills, projects, and people right in front of you and by failing to recognize what you already have. One of the secrets of feeling alive and living extraordinarily is to stop looking for satisfaction somewhere else. Hunt for gratitude wherever you are.

Think thankfulness.

Speak appreciation.

Show gratitude.

Spreading the Gratitude Attitude

One of the greatest ways you can express gratitude and deepen your own sense of purpose is to give back with a generous heart. When someone asks you for help, be grateful you *get to* versus looking at it as a *have-to* situation. Offer an assist without someone having to ask you first. Do something anonymously to support someone else's dreams. When another person feels discouraged or let down, remind them that if this is the worst thing that happens, it's been a good day. Teach others how to keep an intentional attitude of gratitude at the forefront of their thinking.

Human beings were not created to be alone, and a little appreciation goes a long way in showing love to your fellow man or woman. Not only will you lift someone else up, but your very expression of thanks may indeed be the heart and soul of your own high calling. And don't fail to let others show their appreciation for you.

I can think of no deeper sadness than to achieve everything you dreamed of, only to find yourself alone with no one to share your accomplishments with. Sometimes I just want to yell at people, "For Pete's sake, take a moment to celebrate your hard work, and show appreciation to the people who helped you accomplish your goals."

In our twenty-first-century society, not many feel valued in our hustle-and-bustle world. So when you spread sunshine in the form of acknowledgment, you make a meaningful difference. We've got enough complainers on this planet; set yourself apart. Whether you write it on a sticky note, send it in a text, or tell someone over a meal, spread the gift of expressed gratitude. It does no good to keep thankfulness to yourself. A shift in focus can even help you heal.

MIND, BODY, AND SPIRIT STRENGTHENERS

YOUR ABUNDANT PURPOSE CHALLENGE

When life knocks you down, look hard until you find one person or thing you can feel grateful for. Every. Single. Day.

YOUR ABUNDANT PURPOSE EXERCISE

Become a gratitude journalist. Write down three things daily that you are grateful for and report them to someone else. Share your gratitude perspective with a child, grandchild, niece, or nephew on an ongoing basis—make it your special thing, and teach them gratitude by example. Speak daily gratefulness to your spouse, sibling, parent, friend, or coworker. Tell God what you are grateful for each day; he's never too tired, distracted, or self-absorbed to care about what interests us. He's the one who calls us to a life of intentional thanksgiving.

YOUR ABUNDANT PURPOSE SCRIPTURE

1 Thessalonians 5:18 (NKJV): "In everything give thanks; for this is the will of God in Christ Jesus for you."

YOUR ABUNDANT PURPOSE PROMISE

Gratitude is the catalyst that will empower your purpose.

YOUR ABUNDANT PURPOSE STUDY AND DISCUSSION PROMPTS

Have you noticed how often small children express gratitude, either directly or indirectly? Do you have a childlike heart of gratefulness? If not, what can you do to change that?

Why do you think expressing thanks lifts our moods—even in times of difficulty?

How does an attitude of gratitude directly correlate to experiencing the abundant life Christ promised us?

CHAPTER 11
Made for Healing

Hardship often prepares an ordinary person for an extraordinary destiny.

—Christopher Markus and Stephen McFeely, *The Voyage of the Dawn Treader*

If you are breathing, God has a reason for you to exist on this planet. But I probably don't have to tell you that you are also guaranteed to have some brokenness and trouble in this life (John 16:33). However, brokenness does not mean we have no purpose or that our purpose has been permanently extinguished.

I've come to realize that you cannot experience a miracle unless you first have a problem. So every problem is a potential miracle in the making, and the bigger your problem, the greater your opportunity for a miracle. But we do have responsibility in the process.

Dis-ease (hyphen intentional) will visit us all at some point in life, though it takes different forms for different people. Most of us have either experienced physical, emotional, relational, financial, or spiritual dis-ease or else we will and just don't know it yet. But difficulties need not stunt the fulfillment of God's plans for our lives. Jon Culwell, a veteran who discovered God's abundant purpose beyond the emotional war wounds he sustained, knows this firsthand.

During his final military tour in Iraq, Jon witnessed the horrific, survived the worst, and came home a broken man. Like the beaten traveler in the parable of the Good Samaritan, Jon needed someone to clean and bandage his wounds, carry him to a safe place, and allow him healing rest. But Jon discovered his spirit hungered for attention first before his emotions and body could be restored. In order to heal, he needed people to point him to Jesus.

Escaping the Pain

I met Jon in a local café. Dishes clanked and snippets of conversation wafted from nearby tables, but within minutes, I didn't notice either as Jon and I began to talk about his childhood.

I asked, "When you were a boy, was there anything special you dreamed of doing when you became an adult?"

Jon's eyes instantly glazed with a faraway expression. "When I was little, I wanted to be a fireman, but mostly I wanted to be different from my family. My mom had four kids, and I was the youngest. Things weren't easy, and often they weren't very good at home. From the time I was four until I was thirteen, we moved over a dozen times. We hopped from town to town and state to state."

Jon looked down and played with the edge of a napkin while he spoke. "All my life, I was always the new kid at school, and I hated feeling off balance. It just seemed like something was off with me, though I didn't know what it was. I was hyperactive. I learned to be aggressive and mean. I didn't care about some things I knew I should have. And I justified a lot of behaviors."

My circumstances were completely different from Jon's, but I could also relate to his description of feeling as if something was off. It wasn't lost on me that most people I know have struggled with justification, and I put myself at the top of the list. There have been times when I knew that I needed something but couldn't quite identify what it was. I may not always understand my own pain, but like Jon, I will do what I can to escape it.

Jon's forehead furrowed and his hands stopped moving. "When I was thirteen, I moved out and started making my own way."

"At thirteen?" I repeated.

He nodded and continued his story matter-of-factly. "I had already learned how to look tough, and I could make people laugh, so that helped me survive a lot. I ended up in foster homes for a little bit, but then I got in trouble with the law and had to go to military school at fifteen years old. This may sound weird, but I fell in love with the structure and discipline of military life. I enjoyed waking up in the morning and making my bed. I liked having someone start my day with exercise. I'd never had a regimen before. For me, it was fun."

I correlated his feelings to things I'd learned. In my younger years, I avoided discipline, seeing it as a negative. But I too discovered that something as simple as making my bed every morning infused me with a sense of satisfaction and spurred me on to bigger things. A sense of order provides a soothing balm to a weary soul and energy for the spirit.

Jon continued. "At eighteen, I joined the military. I was deployed three times in six years. Then on June 4, 2009, our convoy was hit by an RKG-3 anti-tank hand grenade. A buddy of mine, a medic, sustained major wounds to his right arm and left leg, so I hurried up and tied a tourniquet, hoping to stop his blood loss until help arrived. But nothing could have saved him. After nineteen hours, he passed away."

My eyes welled, envisioning myself in Jon's shoes. I could almost feel the heat of the desert sun and taste the sandy dust choking the air as Jon helplessly fought to keep his friend alive. And yet, I knew nothing I could conjure in my mind compared to what Jon felt.

He soldiered on with his story. "When I returned stateside after getting out of the military, I dabbled a little with drugs. I wanted to make the memories and the pain go away. But that didn't work very well. I eventually took a civilian job for the state department as an explosives detector and canine handler, going back overseas for about four years."

Intrigued, I said, "What did this civilian job do for you?"

Jon cocked his head for several seconds before speaking. "Well, everyone wants to do something they're good at. Nobody wants to play tennis if they're a basketball player. This kind of work came pretty easy for me, and I liked it."

He didn't consciously take the job to protect someone else from going through what his buddy did. Jon just saw it as an opportunity to make a lot of money doing what he liked in a place far from regular life.

"I woke up, worked long hours, dropped into bed, then started over the next day. I was too busy to think—until I was injured and they ended my contract."

I wondered what the plane ride back to US soil must have felt like for Jon. What went through his mind, knowing he could no longer hide in his career? A lot of people try to heal their invisible wounds through work or other obsessions.

Jon said, "When I came back home, I couldn't find a job for anything over minimum wage, and depression kicked in. I immediately looked for something to mask it all, and this time found it in drug use. I had all these bottled-up emotions, all the stuff I'd avoided feeling that was burning inside me, so even though using drugs was just a temporary fix, I didn't care. They seemed to help until they made things worse. I didn't realize it yet, but the devil wanted to keep me down so I couldn't be the man God wanted me to be. Addiction provides a way for him to take people who are already broken and break them even more."

Jon scooted his chair closer to the table. "A wise man once told me, 'Being an addict is like being in your underwear when it's ten degrees outside and the wind is howling. The devil puts a nice warm blanket on you called addiction. For the moment, you feel comfortable, you don't have to think about anything. But then he rips the blanket away.' That's what it's like when the effects of your addiction stop numbing you. The cold feels ten times colder because you enjoyed that short-lived warmth."

I considered how Jon's experience compared to what others have shared with me. The specifics of his PTSD, depression, and addictions were different from a lot of people's stories, but the feelings he described were similar. Every painful situation makes us look for something to ease our suffering. And if we aren't careful, what we choose to cope with our pain can numb or even paralyze us, making an abundant life impossible.

Overcoming the Things That Inhibit Your Purpose

Three dis-eases can cause emotional shutdown, preventing us from fulfilling all we were made for:

- Feeling confused or uncertain what our unique giftings, talents, and abilities are.
- Feeling unworthy, unusable, and unforgivable.
- Feeling debilitated by physical, relational, financial, emotional, or spiritual trials.

The good news is, recognizing the lies that damage us, the deceptions that make us feel confused and unworthy, can lead us to God's truth. God doesn't want us hurt, damaged, or debilitated. He wants to heal us from our dis-ease so we can live our lives fully (Ps. 103:2–5).

If you'll allow him, our Father in heaven will even use your pain to help you fulfill your purpose. Second Corinthians 1:4 reminds us, "He comforts us in all our troubles so that we can comfort others. When they are troubled, we will be able to give them the same comfort God has given us."

Because of what I've lived through, I am convinced that pain can be either a poison or a potion for finding and experiencing all God wants for us—depending on how we react to it. This may sound crazy to you now, but consider this: just because your life is dark right now, don't assume you've been buried. Believe you've been planted. When you feel covered up by adversity, start dropping positive seeds and let them take root. You may not see a sprout of movement for a while, but that doesn't mean nothing is happening below the surface. Faith is God's catalyst not only for lasting healing but also for finding the high calling we were made for. Many a purpose is unearthed through pain. A recent conversation reminded me of this truth.

The summer heat and humidity quickly dissipated from my conscious mind as I listened to a friend in the raw stage of a cancer diagnosis. Her lament wasn't over her condition but her guilt.

"Now that I'm going through this, I realize what I've done to people, especially some of my family members who had cancer before me. I didn't visit them like I should have. When they tried to talk to me about how they felt, I threw a few platitudes their way but didn't really listen to what was on their heart." Heavy tears rolled off her flushed cheeks as she spoke.

I took her hand in mine. "Give yourself the kind of grace Jesus offers you," I said. "Before I nearly died in the hospital all those years ago, and went through other trials, I didn't have the level of understanding and compassion I have for the hurting now. I didn't know what I didn't know. I wanted to understand, but without experiencing those deeper levels of pain, I had no idea how hard life could be in certain seasons. I used to beat myself up, but then I learned that because of what the pain taught me, God gave me the desire and purpose of reaching out and showing care to those who are sick or going through a difficult time. But first I had to walk through some dark valleys myself."

My friend's smile removed some of the sadness from her eyes. "I know I should have more faith. After all, God won't give me any more than I can handle."

I chuckled, and then apologized. "I'm sorry for laughing, but people misquote that all of the time. There is actually no Scripture verse that says God won't give us more than we can handle. I think he absolutely will. When we are overwhelmed, helpless, and at our wit's end, we understand how much we need him; otherwise, we'd foolishly keep trying to do life on our own."

"I never thought about it like that," my friend said.

I stroked her hand lightly. "Tough times can teach all of us great lessons. None of us wants to go through them, but I can tell you from experience, you become more approachable to people in need when you've come through adversity yourself. I understand the guilt you describe because you feel like you failed people previously. But forgive yourself, and ask God to show you how not to make the same mistake in the future.

"If you allow God to work through you, from this point forward you will have a fresh perspective and new purpose. You will encourage and lend a supportive hand in ways you never could before. And when you are focused on honoring God and helping others, you'll find little time for dwelling on the past or fretting about the future.

"I can assure you, there will be moments when you feel lonely, afraid, or inept. Write down Deuteronomy 31:6, and keep it with you to combat whatever threatens to hold you back. And remember, when everyone else is busy, God is never preoccupied—his attention is on you and your needs. Even while you're walking through this difficult season, ask God to give you a glimpse into his grander purpose for you, already at work."

In spite of the cancer, God is already using my friend in a mighty way, although she rarely sees the fullness of her own impact. When she shows up for church, we see her strength. When she smiles in spite of her circumstances, we see her hope. When she repeats God's promises found in Scripture, we see her faith. When she comforts others in their hurts, we see a beautiful purpose as God uses her to demonstrate his caring love.

For any of us, an inner sense of unworthiness creates its own dis-ease. Do you ever feel like you aren't capable?

Feeling Unworthy

There are those of us who know what we're meant to do, but because of life's circumstances we feel unworthy, unusable, and unforgivable. We decide we are no good and therefore can do no long-term good. Unless we heal from the damage, we can never live out our God-designed purpose. But the good news is that *your* opinion of you doesn't determine your value; who God says you are decides your worth. If you've made mistakes and sinned, or if others have told you you're less-than, welcome to the world the rest of us inhabit! Allow God to forgive you, heal you, and use you. Let him show you how he can even use the thing about you that you think is so inferior or terrible to enhance the power of your purpose. (By now you understand I'm speaking from experience!)

Transparency and authenticity are tremendously motivating and encouraging to those who need hope, or who feel as if their mess-ups are somehow worse than those the rest of us make. A willingness to share your story will not only provide deeper healing for you but can help others heal as well.

If you feel unusable, ask God to show you how he sees you, after you've asked Jesus to cover your sins. It might surprise you to discover that the thing that makes you cringe is what makes you appealing to other people when you humble yourself and reveal your soul.

Every human being is a fragile vessel made of clay (2 Cor. 4:7). Some of us are even cracked pots. But when we allow the light of Christ's forgiveness to shine through our broken places, a beautiful prism shines into the world. An exceedingly abundant purpose comes from the reflection of *all* our parts, not just the pretty ones.

Recovering from Afflictions

But sometimes the aftermath of life's trials block us from experiencing the abundance Christ offers. Afflictions come in all forms, any of which can make us vulnerable to paralysis. However, no matter what our condition, we can find a way to make a difference, enhance our own healing, and touch others in meaningful ways.

Some people's physical conditions limit their mobility and opportunities to interact with others. Perhaps you're one of them. Your purpose may come from reflecting the peace of Christ through your attitude, or by expressing your gratitude to a person who rarely hears positive affirmation.

You may be housebound, but can you encourage people from a computer? In a crowd of people screaming on blogs and social media, you could provide a calming influence.

Who's coming to visit you? If you have caregivers and support people, they could probably use ongoing encouragement. Those who pour so much of themselves out often need a refill. Who can you pour into?

Your body may not operate well, even preventing your fingers from typing, your ears from hearing, or your voice from speaking—but can you pray? God can read your thoughts, and he can still use you in a mighty way when you call on him for the benefit of others.

Perhaps it isn't physical healing you need but relational healing. Healing damaged relationships requires two consistently willing people. If the other person is unwilling to help you fix the damage, then pray for him or her continually. And do for someone else what you wish you could do for the person who refuses to mend fences.

When your finances are crumbling, remember, God owns the cattle on a thousand hills (Ps. 50:10), so we can call on him for every need. But consider: his ways don't always make sense to us, especially when we are in a scary situation. A season of financial famine may be part of a more substantial plan to provide testimony to someone else at a later date. Your current lack might remind you that you can't experience true abundance apart from God. This temporary situation may build lasting faith. Whatever the case, God might stretch you, but he won't abandon you. Our Father in heaven is our true provider (Phil. 4:19). He is the source of all financial healing.

Maybe, as with Jon Culwell, your deepest wounds come from a spiritual hunger camouflaged by emotional pain.

Jon learned that honest vulnerability was crucial to his healing process and helped him find his purpose. His transparency reflected how far he had come. He told me, "A friend talked me into signing up for a men's conference our church was taking the guys to, but the day we were supposed to leave, I went and got high. I showed up late, not expecting anyone to be there, but the van was still in the parking lot. I knew our pastor would tell me to leave when he saw how messed up I was, but he didn't. I couldn't walk or talk straight, but he acted like he didn't notice. I was shocked when he slapped me on the shoulder and told me it was good to see me.

"As soon as I sat down, we drove off. So there I was, in a vehicle full of church guys, high out of my gourd, heading to a Christian men's event. It was crazy.

"At the conference, I felt like each of the speakers was talking directly to me, and an idea began to form in my mind. *My thinking has been off. It's not, Why did God let this happen to me? It should be, What can he do with it if I let him? He didn't cause the evil I've seen and experienced, but he can do something good with it if I open my heart to him.* Everything shifted for me that day."

When Jon got home, he was still doing drugs and drinking, but he started reading an old, tattered Bible. "After my buddy died in Iraq, it bugged me trying to figure out why I survived. There had to be a reason, right? I kept reading the Bible, and one night I had an epiphany. God tells us exactly what he wants us to do. I just needed to tell other people how my relationship with Jesus healed me and helped me start feeling alive again."

Slowly, Jon turned his life around. And today he no longer lives in shame, fear, or drug use. "When I open my eyes, I say, 'Thank you, God, for the day you've given me. Thanks for the chance to do good things and for showing me what they are. We both know I'll mess up today, so thanks ahead of time for forgiving me. I don't deserve your grace and mercy, but I am grateful.' When I began living for God, I felt like I came back to life."

A Redeeming Date

Jon Culwell didn't make the connection when the calendar was first set, but it didn't take long for it to hit him. On June 4, 2017, Jon was baptized—exactly eight years to the day from when he lost his friend in Iraq. It was no coincidence; it was part of God's coordinated healing plan. June 4 is no longer his regret date; it's his redeemed date.

It is not time that heals all wounds. It is what God does through time that heals us. God is still in the miracle business, but the real miracle may be in how he uses us in spite of our conditions.

What amazing purpose is in store for you? What is coming in the next hour that you don't yet see? What will he restore if you allow him? Consider your circumstances in light of some stories many of us are familiar with.

When the children of Israel were backed up against the Red Sea, God parted the waters and gave them a dry path—but they had to pick up their belongings and walk (Exod. 14:15–21). If a broken relationship backed you into a corner, do you need to pick up your pride and walk toward reconciliation, allowing God to heal both the other person and yourself?

When their enemies were going to wipe out the Jewish people, God saved them from imminent doom—but Queen Esther had to risk her life by approaching the king to ask for a pardon (Esther 4:10–14). If you have made a monumental mistake and feel doomed, should you confess your sin to God and other believers, demonstrate your willingness to make things right, and ask for mercy, so that God can restore your spirit as well as your reputation?

When David faced Goliath, God gave the young boy favor to save a nation—but the boy still had to pick up five smooth stones and fling one at the giant (1 Sam. 17:40, 49). If you've cowered in fear, do you need to grab some courage, consult God about your next steps, and take action so you can slay the enemies of your future?

God is not stifled by your circumstances. The only thing that stifles him is your unwillingness to believe and accept his good plan for your life. He desires to give good things to you as much as he does to others; those promises in the Bible are yours too. When times get tough, you don't have to keep up appearances. Give yourself permission to be human and fall into the arms of God when life gives you more than you can handle.

There is no prayer guaranteed to keep us from sickness or provide us with wealth, nor any promise that God will give us everything we want. So how should you pray when you're betrayed, or hurt, or confused, or in great pain? Ask God to give you the endurance to fight and overcome, especially in your most difficult moments. When we lean into him, even our weaknesses become strengths (2 Cor. 12:9–10).

Allowing Yourself to Heal

As you read the Bible, you will see that Jesus was tired, Jesus was poor, Jesus was betrayed, Jesus was abandoned, Jesus was tortured, and ultimately, Jesus was murdered. Yet when Jesus endured the troubles of life—something he promised us we'd also face—he prayed and accepted his Father's plan.

Take a look at Jesus's prayer in John 12:27: "Now my soul is deeply troubled. Should I pray, 'Father, save me from this hour'? But this is the very reason I came!"

Facing the cross, Jesus took his pain to God the Father—not to dishonor, blame, or disobey his Father, but simply for Jesus to present his personal anguish and express his feelings.

You too can be honest with God. He can take it. Tell him how you feel. Say, "God, I'm troubled. I'm really struggling right now. I'm hurting very badly. I want this to go away." It's okay to say those things. Jesus did. But also be willing to accept a plan beyond what you might see in the moment.

Avoidance only extends our pain, no matter the origin of our hurts. Sometimes problems exist to show us God's great miracles, but we have to take part in the process. If you fall eleven times, get up twelve, then ask God to restore you to your abundant purpose.

Living in a bar, dying for your next drug hit, numbing yourself through gluttony, craving your next shopping spree, hungering for your next morsel of gossip—none of this is living at all. It's barely existing. You were not created to subsist on the scraps of an unconscious life. You were made for so much more.

You don't have to fight to feel special, appreciated, or deeply loved. You already are those things—you simply may not know it yet. Your Father in heaven sees past your flaws. In his eyes, you are the unique, wonderful, and talented person he handcrafted. You are wanted and treasured like no one else who has ever existed or ever will. He made you with significant plans in mind. It's up to you to live them out.

If you don't know what gifts, abilities, or purpose God gave you, then follow Jon Culwell's example and meditate on the Bible, and keep asking and seeking until he reveals his plan for your life. It's never too late for a fresh start with fresh faith. One of the most powerful healing agents I've found comes from pursuing our God-designed reason for existence.

Exercise Now Faith: praise God in advance for revealing your purpose and showing you how to live it out. Wait with watchful eyes, open ears, a teachable spirit, and a believing heart. When you do, your life will begin to display outwardly what he's prepared inside you.

MIND, BODY, AND SPIRIT STRENGTHENERS

YOUR ABUNDANT PURPOSE CHALLENGE

Pain can make us forget what we were created for. Remember, you were created on purpose, with purpose, to fulfill an abundant purpose. But nothing gets better until you admit something is wrong, so acknowledge your hurts and free yourself to heal.

YOUR ABUNDANT PURPOSE EXERCISE

Each day, search for a Scripture promise to help you through tough moments or triggering situations. Then log it in your gratitude journal, where you can keep a record of all God's personal promises to you.

YOUR ABUNDANT PURPOSE SCRIPTURE

Ephesians 2:10 (TLB): "It is God himself who has made us what we are and given us new lives from Christ Jesus; and long ages ago he planned that we should spend these lives in helping others."

YOUR ABUNDANT PURPOSE PROMISE

Healing often reveals your greater purpose, hidden in the restoration process.

YOUR ABUNDANT PURPOSE STUDY AND DISCUSSION PROMPTS

Do you believe your hurts matter? Your excitement matters? Your anticipation matters? Any God-given emotion you feel matters to the One who made you. Did you know he sees you—and he loves what he sees?

How has God already shaped a crown of beauty, or shown you an abundant purpose, out of the ashes of your past pain?

Are you weighed down by anger, resentment, jealousy, hatred, unforgiveness, or self-justification? Are you trying to numb out or avoid feelings? What past do you need to shed so you can fly freely into your Christ-promised future?

CHAPTER 12
Made for Fruitfulness

Sow an act—reap a habit: sow a habit—reap a character: sow a character—reap a destiny.

—Charles Ellicott, *A New Testament Commentary for English Readers*

Abundance as defined by *Merriam-Webster* includes this description: a "relative degree of plentifulness."[1] It defines *prosperity*, a synonym of *abundance*, as "the condition of being successful or thriving; *especially:* economic well-being."[2] Is this what Jesus meant when he promised to give us life to the full?

Jesus does promise us abundance. The word he uses for it in John 10:10 comes from the Greek word *perissos*. Look up this word in *Strong's Concordance* and you'll get a feel for its lavish nature. It involves excess, an exceeding of expectations, an outstripping of the normal limit—in short, it's a "more than" word.[3] That's *perissos* abundance! And then there's its cousin, *huperekperissou*, translated as follows in Ephesians 3:20: "Now to Him who is able to do *exceedingly abundantly* above all that we ask or think . . ." (NKJV, emphasis mine). What does that long, complicated word *huperekperissou* mean? "Superabundantly"![4] According to God's Word, we are promised superabundance.

When we hear the word *abundance*, most of us immediately envision monetary wealth or possessions. So when it comes to fulfilling an exceedingly abundant purpose, many of us assume our bank account will be flush with funds, we'll drive higher-end vehicles, and if we do really well, we might score a vacation home in one of our favorite places.

But you and I both know wealthy people who are dissatisfied, unhappy, and downright miserable. And we know folks who constantly struggle to make the rent or mortgage or put enough food on the table for their kids and yet are inexplicably content, happy, and downright joyful. And to make things all the more interesting, we know wealthy people who are joyful and poor families who are bitter.

It's clear that abundant life has little to do with money. Riches come in many forms. Like the apostle Paul, whether we have much or little, we can learn the secret to living a truly prosperous life (Phil. 4:11–13). There is a power source that gives us this ability.

Galatians 5:22–23 tells us that "the fruit of the Spirit is love, joy, peace, forbearance, kindness, goodness, faithfulness, gentleness and self-control. Against such things there is no law" (NIV).

Now that sounds like a superabundant life we'd all like to live.

But we all know people who are sour and cantankerous. Even those who believe in Jesus don't always appear fruitful. I often have to check myself by asking this question: Does my life demonstrate the fruit of Galatians 5? Sometimes I don't like my honest answer. What about you? If you don't like what you see upon self-examination, look a little closer at two vital—and often overlooked—points in this passage.

First and most important, the fruit isn't the fruit of the believer—it's the fruit of the Spirit. *He* is the power source that enables us to live with abundance. If we aren't listening to God through study and contemplation or talking to God through prayer and worship, we're powerless.

Also, did you pick up on that tiny word "and" at the end of the fruit list: ". . . faithfulness, gentleness *and* self-control" (emphasis mine)? This tells us that our life should mirror every element noted—not perfectly but consistently. We are not to pick and choose or justify having one or two fruitful traits while we're deficient in the rest. However, neither should we beat ourselves up for what we lack. Weakness is merely an opportunity to exercise humility, to allow God's strength to fill our cracks and let Christ's light cover our flaws.

So how do we instill the nine distinct parts of the fruit of God's Holy Spirit in our lives? What practical changes will provide us with more pleasure and make us more pleasant to be around? Where do we go if we want a superabundant life? It's simpler than you might think—but I'm not going to promise it will be easy.

Harvesting the Fruit of the Spirit

When we review the nine aspects of the fruit of God's Spirit individually, we begin to better understand the fullness we were made for.

1. Love: I've learned that love is an active verb more than a warm, fuzzy noun. Love means doing something to demonstrate acceptance and appreciation, *especially* when you don't feel it. Nothing we do matters unless love is a decision we make and the driving force behind our motives. When we love in faith, the feelings will eventually follow.

2. Joy: Deciding to live in joy comes much easier when you focus on gratitude. Concentrating on the good attributes of a person or the potential of a project helps you move through the painful periods. Remember, you *get* to do life. Praising God as well as praying to him instills you with joy that splashes onto those around you.

3. Peace: We experience peace when we feel whole. No thing and no person can fulfill you like a relationship with Jesus and the indwelling of God's Holy Spirit. When you stop chasing what's out there and plug into his presence inside you, you will experience less stress and more calm.

4. Forbearance: Sometimes it takes study, practice, and biblical self-talk to restrain yourself and tolerate the way other people choose to exercise their free will. After all, you are not God. Other people are *his* business; what they choose is between him and them. When you remind yourself that Christ had to die on the cross for you and why your daily mistakes would nail him there again and again, it will help you see others through his eyes of patience and empathy.

5. Kindness: Think kindly, speak kindly, and act kindly, regardless of how you feel. The more you practice kindness, the more natural it becomes. Slow down and have a conversation with an elderly person. Take groceries or a prepared meal to a family going through a hard time. Offer the harried clerk a smile and sincere compliment. Ask for a manager to tell them something good. Share with someone why they make a difference in your life. Small acts of kindness can completely transform another person and fill your spirit with warmth.

6. *Goodness:* Put someone else's needs ahead of your own—whether they appreciate it or not, and even if they don't notice. Choose to do excellent work, not just enough to get by. Do the hard, right thing versus taking the easy way out. The sense of accomplishment you feel when choosing well, especially when the follow-through is difficult, will infuse you with energy when you live life selflessly.

7. *Faithfulness:* Temptation visits us all, but you do not have to act on it. Seduction can make you sweat, but nothing you give in to will ever compare with how you feel when you overcome. Don't wait until temptation knocks on your heart's door. Decide in advance to remain true to God and the people you love. Maybe no one but you and God will ever know what you avoided, but your satisfaction will increase your peace.

8. *Gentleness:* Few things are as difficult as returning good for evil or turning your cheek when someone seems to slap you in the face. But like Jesus, we can pray, "Father, forgive them, for they don't know what they are doing" (Luke 23:34). Just as a whisper grabs our attention more than a scream, when our gentleness is evident to all, people pay closer attention. Dare to be different. When the world is shouting, show them the glow of Christ's gentleness in you, and feel your stress dissipate.

9. *Self-control: Moderation, discipline, silence, obedience*—these are words we avoid in the twenty-first century. Some think they are old-fashioned, clearly demonstrated on many social media sites where our entitled generation spouts opinions as if they were God's gospel. But people aren't looking for one more person to tell them what they're doing wrong; they are desperately seeking someone who can show them the way

to a better life. When we speak less, listen more, and show the fruit of the Holy Spirit in us through self-control, our influence grows. It goes against instinct, but showing restraint gains the respect and admiration many of us hope for.

Balancing Perfectionism and Effort

Every single day we are faced with the fact that we are weak and unable to practice the fruit of the Spirit flawlessly. The good news is, our weakness reminds us of our need for Jesus.

Not a day goes by that I don't require Christ's friendship, his forgiveness, his acceptance, his teaching, and his unfailing love. No human being, not even my adoring husband, can give me what Jesus can. But I must humble myself to admit my need before I can accept his promise.

Accepting our weaknesses and leaning into God's strength takes the pressure off. Confessing that we can't fix all problems ourselves, that we aren't able to control everything, that we don't have what it takes to go at life alone, is freeing.

But our weaknesses don't absolve us from the necessity of consistent action. Throughout his Word, God still commands us to put our faith in motion. And he asks us to constantly evaluate our words and behaviors. One way to see if you are bearing the fruit of the Holy Spirit is to ask yourself why you do things. If it's for pats on the back, then your motives are off. Consider these words of Jesus:

> Be careful not to practice your righteousness in front of others to be seen by them. If you do, you will have no reward from your Father in heaven.
>
> So when you give to the needy, do not announce it with trumpets, as the hypocrites do in the synagogues and on the streets, to be honored by others. Truly I tell you, they have received their reward in full. But when you give to the needy, do not let your left hand know

> what your right hand is doing, so that your giving may be in secret. Then your Father, who sees what is done in secret, will reward you. (Matt. 6:1–4 NIV)

In other words, when displaying the fruit of God's Spirit, don't steal your own superabundant blessings by doing it for self-glorification. Pray anonymously. Gift anonymously. Serve anonymously. Send cards, letters, or notes anonymously. Give God the credit—then enjoy the intrigue, the thrill, the pleasure of doing something for someone else as a secret between you and your heavenly Father.

Anonymous acts encompass the entirety of the fruit of the Holy Spirit, and when we are authentically focused on others, not only do they benefit, but we ourselves experience the superabundance we were made for. Whether we are financially wealthy or money poor, nothing feels as rich and satisfying as living fully bearing the fruit of God's Spirit, using all of its aspects to pour into someone else. Like an electronic device connected to electricity, we come alive and fulfill our purpose when we plug in to the power source of God's Holy Spirit.

Making a Difference Where You Are

While writing this book, I polled friends and followers on social media to ask them what fulfilling your purpose meant to them. I appreciated what a retired teacher and librarian named Dee Dee had to say: "I think the key to finding your purpose is different for all of us. I knew from a very early age that I wanted to be a teacher and help kids love school as much as I did."

Dee Dee spent nineteen years in a variety of teaching positions. She loved it. But then she was assigned to be the high school librarian and teach a new class. She wrote:

> It was like coming home. I stayed in that position for the last twelve years of my teaching career. I found my

> purpose by helping the students that others gave up on. Those who found themselves in situations that would compromise their education: pregnancy, homelessness, attendance issues, etc. I dealt with all of it.
>
> While I was there, I knew how fulfilling it was for me, but when I retired, I found out how much it meant to my students, their parents, siblings, and many others. I received nice messages, notes, cards, and even gifts. One of my favorites came from a young couple. The story won't start out sounding good, but stick with me.
>
> I had helped prepare them for their high school graduation tests. But before they could find out the results, they were stopped for speeding, and both were incarcerated for having drugs in their possession. While they were in jail, I got a message to them that they had each passed.

The couple had graduated while still in jail! But that good news was not the end of Dee Dee's experience with them. Surprises awaited her when she saw them next.

> In my last year of teaching, on graduation day, this young couple showed up. They had both graduated from college and earned degrees. They had relocated to another state and had great careers. They had an adorable child. Personally and professionally, they were doing well.
>
> They left a note on my desk and thanked me for believing in them and helping. They said they would not be where they were without my guidance. After the graduation ceremony, they found me, and we hugged and cried together.
>
> I don't have children of my own, so I can only

> imagine that the pride I felt at that moment is what parents feel. To this day, I love hearing and seeing all my students have accomplished. Their successes tell me I found my purpose.
>
> Do I feel I have completed my purpose now that I've retired? No! There is still another purpose waiting for me to find it. I believe we each have more than one purpose—whether it is in a career or as a person.
>
> I helped over seventy students graduate, who probably would not have. Many have gone on to college, some entered the military, others joined the workforce. Seeing how your own purpose helped others is very humbling. I loved what I did and wish I would have been at the high school longer, but I think part of the reason I am not still there is to allow someone else to find their purpose. I'm passing it on. The new librarian has thanked me for helping to push her into taking the position and is finding it just as rewarding as I did. God puts us where we need to be.

In whatever capacity she is acting, Dee Dee is someone who inspires. She breathes in God's Spirit and exhales it onto the people placed in her path. She would never say this about herself, but I know people who would agree that she is loving, joyful, peaceful, forbearing, kind, good, faithful, gentle, and self-controlled. The fruit of God's Spirit is evident in her life.

Dee Dee lives on purpose, with purpose. And so, throughout the different stages of her life, she has fulfilled her God-given purpose by making the most of every opportunity to give to and act on behalf of others. She has discovered the secret to mastering a life that overflows with rich meaning: through God's Spirit in her, she pours into others wherever she goes.

We don't need a teaching degree to follow Dee Dee's motivating example:

- Accept people, flaws and all. Love others as Christ loves us: mercifully, gracefully, passionately, faithfully, and unconditionally.
- Spread the gift of happiness. I can't think of a more meaningful life than to splatter the fullness of God's Spirit onto as many people as you can, as often as you have opportunity.
- Commit to exceed. We commonly hear the phrase "Exceed customer expectations," but make it your goal to excel, surpass, and transcend the expectations of every person you interact with in extraordinary ways.
- Recognize that you are placed where and when you are, with the people you are with, for a reason (Acts 17:26). Make the most of every conversation, occasion, and circumstance, especially those that might allow you to shine light into someone else's darkness.

The Impact of Spiritual Fruit

You will view the end of your life by what you did during your most vital years—likely, by what you are doing today. Are you pouring into others? Does your life overflow with the fruit of God's Spirit? How will people remember you when you are gone?

Before we can make a difference beyond ourselves, we would do well to remember that what we carry inside will become visible to those around us. Are we the type of people we would like to be around? When others come in close contact, our presence will either sour or sweeten their lives and reveal whether we love or hate ourselves deep inside. Inviting and cultivating the Spirit of God makes a superabundant harvest possible.

I agree with Dee Dee: the key to finding our purpose is different for all of us. But allowing the Holy Spirit to guide us will ensure we eventually find our way to our true destiny. Too often we measure success or abundance through money or position. We think we need to do one thing, and one thing only, to make a difference. But we were made to tend to people and pass on blessings many times over. We were created to share the fruit of God's Spirit with others as often and in as many places as we are planted.

Excitement, passion, adventure, and drive—these are some of the surprising benefits of listening to God and following his plans. We were made for more than a ho-hum existence; we were made for the fullness of a powerful purpose.

MIND, BODY, AND SPIRIT STRENGTHENERS

YOUR ABUNDANT PURPOSE CHALLENGE

An inspiring life is a purpose-filled life. Don't squelch God's Spirit in you, but instead, determine to let it shine on those you come in contact with.

YOUR ABUNDANT PURPOSE EXERCISE

Consider how you sound to others. When you answer the phone, are you grumpy or cheerful? Does your voice reflect happiness or impatience? However you would like people to respond to you, begin to give that treatment first. Radiate God's Spirit, and it will be reflected to you in return.

YOUR ABUNDANT PURPOSE SCRIPTURE

John 4:24 (NASB): "God is spirit, and those who worship Him must worship in spirit and truth."

YOUR ABUNDANT PURPOSE PROMISE

You exist to bear fruit grown through God's Spirit.

YOUR ABUNDANT PURPOSE STUDY AND DISCUSSION PROMPTS

What traits of yours have already contributed to your purpose? What abilities haven't you used?

How are you actively seeking and asking the Holy Spirit for direction to discover your true purpose in life?

Do you fear that following God will be boring or make you feel caged? Why do you think people believe a life of obedience is a bad thing while out-of-control living is more attractive?

CHAPTER 13
Made for Power

When God is involved, anything can happen.

—Charles Swindoll, *Growing Strong in the Seasons of Life*

I was in my younger years and trying to assemble my new office chair, a project complicated by my lack of mechanical skill. *Why are you such an idiot?* I chided myself as a bolt slipped out of my hands for the third time and rolled across the floor. *You're so stupid. You'll never figure this out.*

Then it hit me. I was saying things to myself that I would never say to a child or a friend.

Why?

Why do we engage in such verbal self-abuse?

Self-talk is one of the most crucial factors in determining whether we will live a life of meaning or mediocrity. What we say to ourselves can strengthen or weaken us. Words have the power to harm or to heal depending on how we wield them—especially the words we say to ourselves.

Too often our words tear down what God wants to build up and do through us. Our words shape our decisions, propelling us to pursue our purposes—or causing us to cower and miss out on miraculous outcomes. What we say to ourselves, what we call ourselves, matters, especially in times of uncontrollable challenges.

The Power of Knowing Who You Are

I was a child the first time I heard of the three young Hebrew men. My eyes were glued to the minister's waving hands as they mirrored the historical drama surrounding those youths. It would take years before I dug deeper into the details and learned just how significant these ancient heroes were.

According to *Strong's Concordance*, the birth names of the three boys in English translations were Hananiah, meaning "Yah has been gracious";[1] Mishael, meaning "Who is what God is?";[2] and Azariah, meaning "Yah has helped."[3]

Talk about some powerful names! Yahweh, or more literally, YHVH, means "I Am" or "The Source," while El is another name of God that describes his might, strength, and power.[4] We'll talk about the significance of this information shortly, but first, let me tell you why you may already be familiar with this miraculous account.

These three Hebrew boys are better known to some of us by the names assigned to them by their Chaldean slave masters. There were surely times when Shadrach, Meshach, and Abednego might have felt as if their lives had no special purpose. After all, what difference could slaves make?

Especially when their identities were stripped away. In a time when the meanings of names were taken very seriously, Hananiah's name was changed to Shadrach, thought to mean "Command of Aku" (the moon god); Mishael's to Meshach, likely meaning "Who is as Aku is?"; and Azariah's to Abednego, which may mean "Slave of the god Nebo/Nabu."

If you look closely, you will see the similarity between the Hebrew and Chaldean definitions, with one very important distinction. Yah, Yahweh, and El, names attributed to our one true God, were replaced with the names of demigods. Make no mistake, the Chaldeans were intent on removing the identity and God-given purpose of their captives. Changing their names removed the constant reminder of God's promises to the boys and made them more vulnerable to pagan plans.

When reading some of these historical accounts, it's easy to overlook the depth of the experience and miss the relevance to our own lives. Imagine yourself a young child, probably in your early teens, torn away from home, relocated, renamed, and told to worship a statue or risk death.

Everything you've been taught says there is only one true God, and a statue isn't him. When everyone else bows, you and your two friends remain standing. It's obvious you are violating the king's orders. His guards—big, burly, armed men—start walking toward you.

King Nebuchadnezzar is not a happy man. Three young upstarts have ignored his command. How would you feel hearing him say to you, "Is it true, Shadrach, Meshach, and Abednego, that you refuse to serve my gods or to worship the gold statue I have set up? I will give you one more chance to bow down and worship the statue I have made when you hear the sound of the musical instruments. But if you refuse, you will be thrown immediately into the blazing furnace. And then what god will be able to rescue you from my power?" (Dan. 3:14–15).

A blazing furnace? Surely the unwavering faith of the three young men butted against natural human fear when their refusal to bow down was met with the king's massive wrath. His face distorted with rage, Nebuchadnezzar commanded that the furnace be heated seven times hotter than usual. Then he ordered some of the strongest men in his army to bind Shadrach, Meshach, and Abednego and throw them into the inferno.

How would you have felt in those heart-stopping moments? Some of the king's toughest soldiers died from simply nearing the monstrous flames, yet Hananiah, Mishael, and Azariah did not budge and they did not bow. Think about it. Would you have had their tenacity and boldness to stay true to your call under those conditions?

The three young men had no idea how their story would end. But I think they were given the power to stand in the face of certain death. I think the secret lies in the power-promise hidden in each of their authentic names. Hananiah's name would remind him that God, the great I Am, is always gracious, in good times and in bad. A few definitions stood out to me when I looked up the word *gracious*: pleasing, acceptable, merciful, compassionate, and generous of spirit.[5] Knowing God's commitment to him, Hananiah dedicated himself to please God and make his life acceptable only to him.

When you're struggling with life's circumstances, do you continually rehearse the bad things that have happened? Or, as Hananiah's name suggests, do you remind yourself that the Lord is gracious, merciful, and compassionate? Do you commit to a God who is committed to you?

I find it fascinating that Mishael's name asks, "Who is what God is?" In other words, "Who is as mighty, strong, and powerful as God?" This young man surely thought, *God, the great I Am, is with you, Mishael.* No matter what happened, he knew he was not alone or unprotected. And if you are a believer, you too belong to the almighty God, and can rest in the safeguarding of his arms. So think deeply: Do you know what God is? Do you know you belong to him?

Finally, Azariah's name reinforces the importance of believing before you see. Note the past-tense statement in his name: "Yah has helped." Azariah could reflect on what God had already done for him prior to that moment, and he could praise him in advance of what he boldly believed God was willing to do in his present circumstance. Azariah's name declares Now Faith. As you experience moments of doubt, times when you seem only to fail, rehearse the times and places when God has helped you or others you know. Are you confident in God's willingness to provide a way for you?

Not only did Hananiah, Mishael, and Azariah miraculously survive and step out of the fire, but the awe did not stop there. The high officers, officials, governors, and advisers who crowded around them saw that the fire had not touched them. Not a hair on their heads was singed, and their clothing was not scorched. They didn't even smell of smoke!

How was this possible? There's only one answer.

The Power of Trust in the God Who Calls You

Three young, faith-filled Hebrew boys were created for a purpose that transcended them and time. They belonged to the gracious, mighty, strong, and powerful God who helped them. Facing impossible odds, they saw their purpose clearly and trusted when it made absolutely no sense. They knew that either God would save them from the fire or they would wake up with God on the other side, but either way, they would be rescued. And they were not afraid to say so.

Hananiah, Mishael, and Azariah set an example we can and should follow. When we feel imprisoned or our efforts seem pointless, when life is unfair or we can't seem to get ahead, when we're at a standstill or stuck in the muck, we need to remember that empowerment and abundant purpose come from knowing who we truly are.

What does *your* name mean? Have you researched the definition and considered whether you are living up to the characteristics God desires?

Years ago, when I read that Anita means "grace" or "gracious," I was at first amused. In my raw state, I'm clumsy and brash, a natural klutz. But from the day I spotted a small magnetized card showing my name and its meaning, displayed with similar cards at my favorite bookstore, my thinking changed. I bought the card and stuck it in my purse. Learning what my name meant set me on a quest to define myself differently.

For weeks, I periodically pulled the card from my purse and looked at the words "Anita: Full of Grace." That tiny piece of knowledge intrigued me—Anita was meant to be grace-full. Though I wasn't at the time, I knew what I needed to do.

Eventually, I placed the card on my refrigerator, a landing place for many of my prayer reminders. I began asking God to make me true to the meaning of my name.

Over time, I realized God was answering. With a focus on becoming more of the woman God intended me to be, I found myself less impatient, a better listener, with a more forgiving spirit. Every day I am much more grace-filled than I was the day before, and I trust that tomorrow I will display grace even more fully. By speaking God's desires and truths regularly, I have been changed.

Even if your given name doesn't have the meaning you'd hope for (like my first name), God has given you powerful, life-giving names. He calls you the following:

His child (John 1:12)
His friend (John 15:15)
His justified (Rom. 3:24 NIV)
His heir (Rom. 8:17)
His temple (1 Cor. 6:19)
His righteousness (2 Cor. 5:21 NIV)
His free man or woman (Gal. 5:1)

Once armed with the truth, we have the weapons necessary to overcome self-defeat. Transformative power is ever at our disposal.

The Power of Rescripting

When the revelation of my parentage was exposed, my world as I knew it spun upside down. It felt like solid earth was jerked from beneath my feet. Everything good around me was swamped by this seismic news; my life would never be the same. But by then I'd learned how to implement strategies that help a person stand strong when the uncontrollable strikes. Like Hananiah, Mishael, and Azariah, I rescripted my perceptions and self-talk through the power of words originating with God.

Mental lies told me I was an accident, but God's truth told me I was purposefully knitted in my mother's womb (Ps. 139:13–14).

My conception and birth made me feel unworthy of doing anything special. The news caused old subconscious beliefs, habits, and self-destructive behaviors to bubble up, threatening to keep me imprisoned and paralyzed. But the Bible disputed my label of shame and gave me confidence that God hadn't given up on me or revoked his call on my life (Phil. 1:6).

When the shock of my identity wore off, I realized that the inner sense of oddity I'd felt my entire life, when comparing myself to others, was part of God's amazing plan for me. As I lived more fully in who I truly was, I felt happier and more satisfied. And Ephesians 2:10 became a personal promise to me: "We are God's masterpiece. He has created us anew in Christ Jesus, so we can do the good things he planned for us long ago."

There is great power in rehearsing who God says we are versus listening to emotional lies. I've learned some specific strategies for using self-talk in my favor so it cannot destroy my dreams. Practice has cleaned up my mental language and, as a result, my outcomes have improved. The following points have changed my life:

1. I pay attention to what I'm saying to myself versus allowing my subconscious to run wild, affecting my ability to act positively or productively.
2. When I catch a derogatory or self-deprecating thought, I stop it in its tracks and offset it with truth. I ask myself, *Is this accurate and factual, or is it an emotional lie?*
3. I analyze my thoughts to determine their origins. *Am I mentally repeating hurtful things others have said about me? Is this a defense mechanism based on fear of failure or fear of success? Am I undermining my potential because I feel overwhelmed?*
4. I compare what I'm telling myself with what God says about me. I can rescript my life through the power of Scripture. God's Word protects me from self-sabotage.

The Holy Spirit's power is available to all of us, and whether we realize it or not, I believe it is the true force we hunger for. Every day is filled with purpose—sometimes through dreams and desires, sometimes through sheer survival. Whatever is set before us, our faith in action makes it possible for us to do all God has planned. We were made to overcome self-defeat.

The Power to Pursue Your Purpose

Bumps happen when you pursue your abundant purpose. Expect them, but don't turn them into roadblocks that stop your progress. Instead, believe God when he promises to do something astounding with your faith.

Rescript your life with Scripture. When other people make you feel powerless or try to change you, when you catch yourself undermining opportunities through negative self-talk, arm yourself with truth. Who does God say you are?

God, our great I Am, accepts us, cares about us, and is gracious to us. He not only plants dreams inside us but he supports them with a compassionate and generous Spirit. Speak and step out in faith in the power he will provide.

When we accept his invitation for a personal relationship through his Son, Jesus Christ, we belong to God. And the power of the Holy Spirit is readily available to help us become all we are made to be (John 14:15–17). Plug in to the true force that generates supernatural impact beyond time and current circumstance.

"God has helped" is both a reminder of what he has done for us in the past and a call to faith for our future. This phrase urges us to recognize what he's getting ready to do, though we may not know what it is or how he will accomplish it. Praise God in advance for what you haven't experienced yet. Thank him for working to arrange assistance before the help arrives.

Don't hide your light under a basket. Remember who God calls you to be. He has raised you up for a very special purpose. This is your secret power; it's a key to accomplishing an exceedingly abundant life and experiencing the passion you desire.

MIND, BODY, AND SPIRIT STRENGTHENERS

YOUR ABUNDANT PURPOSE CHALLENGE

Pay closer attention to your inner dialogue and alter it when necessary. Don't let anything hold you back—your past, your emotions, your present conditions. Look up the biblical meaning of your name, and believe God's label, not worn-out, undermining mental messages.

YOUR ABUNDANT PURPOSE EXERCISE

Fast and pray, asking God to reveal his plans for you and infuse you with the Holy Spirit's force to act on them. Powerful and unpredictable results happen when we're intentional to fast and pray (Isa. 58:6).

YOUR ABUNDANT PURPOSE SCRIPTURE

Isaiah 40:29–31: "He gives power to the weak and strength to the powerless. Even youths will become weak and tired, and young men will fall in exhaustion. But those who trust in the LORD will find new strength. They will soar high on wings like eagles. They will run and not grow weary. They will walk and not faint."

YOUR ABUNDANT PURPOSE PROMISE

God's good gifts, when accepted, cannot be denied or taken away.

YOUR ABUNDANT PURPOSE STUDY AND DISCUSSION PROMPTS

What names do you call yourself? Do they align with what God says about his beloved children?

Have you looked up the biblical meaning of your name? If so, what does it mean and are you living up to its definition?

Have you ever been faced with an impossible situation, only to see God act miraculously on your behalf? Have you seen him do impossible things for other people? Why do you think faith makes a difference to outcomes?

CHAPTER 14
Made for Legacy

A life is not important except in the impact it has on other lives.
—Jackie Robinson, *I Never Had It Made*

Most of us harbor an inner need to create a legacy. We are designed with a passionate desire to leave an imprint on the world we've inhabited, with hopes that a lasting impression will continue beyond our final breath. But I wonder how many people die without realizing that their frustrations and perceived lack of success are illusions. A lasting impact does not require a large public forum.

In response to a few questions about what purpose means to her, my friend Nancy told me an encouraging story. Those who struggle to believe they have anything extraordinary to offer the world should find inspiration from this true tale.

Less than a month after her mother's passing, Nancy told me,

> You asked about life's purpose, which is what I've been thinking about since the morning Jesus escorted my mom home. Mom lived a very unassuming life, always choosing to work behind the scenes, out of the limelight. This quiet lady was loved by nearly everyone who knew her. I'd often wondered about that, and it caused me to reflect on some of the things she did that she discounted, yet were important to other people. Everything started with the word *why*.

> Why did Mom greet people with a smile and hug when she saw them?
>
> Why were my friends drawn to her?
>
> Why did she do whatever was needed to keep her family clean, clothed, and fed?
>
> Why did community leaders ask her to chair or cochair committees for local activities and charities?
>
> Why was she sought to determine the amount of homemade ice cream for three hundred people during three-day events held in the city park on hot Missouri summer days?
>
> Why did her large kitchen often overflow with oatmeal and chocolate chip cookies for groups big and small?
>
> Why did she pray for people to hear about a man named Jesus who loved them enough to die for them, wanting them to know him in a personal way?
>
> Why did any of these people, plus hundreds of others, reach out to my mom? Why?

After contemplating her mother's life, Nancy came to an insightful conclusion. She said,

> It took me decades to discover the secret of this unassuming woman I was blessed to call Mom. I wasn't stupid or selfish, but during the younger seasons of my life, I didn't appreciate her impact. The answer to all of the whys is that her purpose was to show unconditional love.
>
> Mom lived her purpose in every breath she took. She simply loved—the young and the old, the easy-to-love and the difficult, the ones who already had a relationship

with Jesus and those who hadn't met him yet. Love was God's ultimate plan for her life.

Refining Purpose and Passion

As an outsider viewing the descriptions of Nancy's mom's compulsion to help others, it's easy to see she had a passion for service, though she didn't see it as a gift in herself or even recognize the gift it was to others. And though she was born with passion and raw talent, it took effort and time for her to grow fully into her God-wired destiny.

Nancy said, "My mother was the first to confess loudly and clearly that she wasn't perfect. In her younger years, she didn't love as well as she grew to do with maturity. There were times when she failed to look past a hurt against her family, or when she disliked a person for what she later said were silly reasons. She lost her temper when people didn't carry through on commitments. She lacked patience when she wanted someone to move faster. She was an imperfect woman who never stopped striving to improve."

Over time, it's the practice of a God-given passion that refines our abundant purpose and shapes our legacy. Let's explore what that might look like for us.

When I'm business-coaching, particularly teaching leadership skills, I often take clients through an especially impactful exercise. I ask them to close their eyes and imagine walking into a funeral service. I invite them to think of the scents of roses, lilies, and chrysanthemums and envision the reds, yellows, purples, and oranges of the floral arrangements. With eyes still closed, they note the background of hushed laughter mingled with occasional sniffles, while I mentally guide them toward the casket at the front of the room. As they near the coffin, they lean close to peek in. The face they see is their own.

After giving my clients a few seconds to let that imaginary moment register, I then direct them to see themselves making their way to the back of the room where they take a seat as the service begins. I ask them to consider who might be seated in the room and what kinds of memories and recollections would be shared. How would family, friends, and casual acquaintances describe them? I ask, "Would remembrances of you make people cringe or smile?"

Next I tell them to contemplate who might speak at the service. What would be said of an entire life represented by a few minutes of reflection? Would they feel satisfied or regretful? Would their actions and attitudes today provide something positive to talk about after their death?

As I give my clients permission to open their eyes, I remind them of an important fact. "You still have time to create an ending more in tune with what you want to happen. Every day of your life, you are writing your legacy through your words, your behaviors, your reactions, your approach, your decisions, and your pursuits."

What you do now will determine the impact you make after you are gone, even if you don't fully comprehend just how great it is. According to Nancy, her mom probably never dreamed her passionate service had touched so many.

Making a Lasting Impression

Nancy said, "During her death, Mom taught me one last lesson. She was eighty-six when she passed, which would typically mean only a handful of mourners would come to pay their respects. Many of her family and friends had gone on before her, yet over five hundred people attended Mom's visitation. We shook hands and hugged a stream of people for over four hours without a break."

Nancy continued:

> Through tears, teens told us how much they loved my mom. Some gave a reason, some simply said, "She was a special lady."
>
> Adults of every age came. We were told of acts of kindness Mom had done, lessons Mom's example had taught, things she said that changed a life.

> Everything people told us during visitation proved my mother's worth and highlighted the impression she'd made. Her voice echoed in my spirit as I left the funeral home. I heard her say, "Just love them, Nancy, that's all you have to do. Just love them; they will know him by your love."
>
> At the end of my own life, I only hope to have lived as purposefully as my mother. She learned the concept from the world's greatest teacher, Jesus, who said, "Love the Lord your God with all your heart, soul, mind, and strength. And love your neighbor as yourself."

Discovering Your Most Important Things

Nancy's story makes me wonder about the conclusion of my own life. What are the most important things people will remember about me when I die? Perhaps the questions spurred in my mind by Nancy's inspiring mother can help us all appreciate the gifts and passions God instilled in us at conception. Consider the following:

- *What will people think about me at my funeral?* You can shape their future words by your actions now.
- *What will they say were the most important things I left behind?* By acting out of your God-given passions, you will make many important contributions.
- *Will the projects I worked on have made a difference?* Possibly, depending on how you conduct yourself to get the work done.
- *Will the people I met have found value in our time together?* If you embrace a passion for people and live out God's call on your life, they will.
- *Will my faith have influenced anyone?* Only if you act on it.
- *Will my relationship with Jesus matter to other people?* Unless you mirror him, his impact will merely appear self-serving.

- *Will any of the things I was made for contribute to a life of meaning?* Only if you live out love while you can.

When you contemplate what you will leave behind, it galvanizes you to use your every breath for living with all the gusto you can muster—no matter what stirs your soul. Can't you feel it inside you? Deeper than bone, in the depth of your soul, you know it—you were made for something bigger than self.

Staying True to Your Passions

We all have talent, but without passion it's hard to follow through and create anything of lasting value.

Nancy isn't even sure her mom knew what her purpose was.

"My mother mistakenly thought a life's purpose had to be something grand enough to plaster across billboards or to take out TV ads to announce. She didn't realize her actions plastered love across hearts and announced acceptance to souls.

"A life's purpose can be silent, joyful, somber, compassionate, or caring. Any of these described my mom's unrecognized purpose at various times in her life. She loved whoever God placed in her path, for however long they were with her. It was her passion."

And that passion, though dismissed by Nancy's mom, made a lasting impression that will live long here on earth. She didn't necessarily see how her "little" contributions made a big difference, but because she followed her passion, lives were changed.

Does any of this resonate with you? Have you falsely believed that a lack of limelight detracts from your impact? What are you passionate about and compelled to do that may touch lives beyond your lifetime?

Whatever it is that makes your heart tick with purposeful excitement, especially when focused on contributing to the good of others, chase it enthusiastically. Don't tell yourself that what you do makes no difference. Don't believe your labor is less-than. Don't let anyone take the wind out of your sails. And don't let any obstacle make you quit. Let your passion push you all the way to the finish line.

Whatever it is you are called to, do it with excellence and with a fiery heart of love. Stretch yourself so you can end your life victoriously.

How you view what you do can affect how effective you are and how long your impact lasts. If you are in charge of little human beings as a daycare worker, if you protect as a social worker, if you clean the halls and rooms where children gather, or if you monitor your own kids in your home, do so with extreme care. These are not jobs to discount; they are roles to respect. Pour into the young people you serve with practiced passion.

You are responsible for shaping futures and helping determine how each child will view the world when he or she matures. The power of your words, attitudes, and acts in their presence will influence how that child will treat those they come in contact with throughout life. The foundational education you provide, mingled with the examples you set, will place children on their own path of influence.

You can set them on an optimistic course by not trying to strip away who they are but encouraging them to master their giftings. Cherish your time with them, reminding yourself that God sees each small life and he adores what he sees. While they are in your presence, be their steward, gatekeeper, and biggest fan. If you are wired to help children discover and live out their purpose, you will fulfill your own.

If it's adults you interact with most, remember that every grown person shelters a child inside, and give that man or woman no less than you would a young person. Particularly keep in mind that these adults are God's kids, so fervently treat them with all the respect, support, and appreciation their heavenly Father wants them to receive.

If you serve behind a counter or desk, acknowledge each person you see with warmth and display superior work ethics. If you take care of business behind the scenes in a back office, provide information, create projects, or solve problems, then meet expectations with excellence and a pleasant temperament. If you build on construction sites, do maintenance on machines, or assemble in a factory, look for ways to enjoy the work of your hands.

Whatever you do, strive passionately with God's purpose in mind. Work as unto the Lord (Col. 3:23). Behave the same way as if Jesus were standing beside you, because he is. Honor him in your everyday acts by remembering you have purpose wherever you are placed—and likely your greatest call is to affect others in a beneficial way. Put passion behind your labor; not only will you receive rewards, but you will make the difference you desire.

Every work you are given is a gift. Start your day and begin your projects with this thought: you don't have to do what you do, you *get* to. Keeping this in mind will infuse your actions with energy and provide you with exceptional purpose. Even if you feel alone, undervalued, or challenged by difficulties.

Precautions About Passion

When speaking of passion, I feel like I need to offer a word of warning. Whether we aspire to fulfill big, dreamy goals or complete simple, daily endeavors, our purpose, our passion, and an exceedingly abundant life should not be idolized. Just as we are not to worship created things but our Creator, neither should we exalt our passions over the One who provides us with the joy of feeling alive and allows us to leave a legacy.

It's true we exist on purpose, with purpose, and are meant to fulfill an abundant purpose, but our existence is not all about us. God's plan put into action through our free will—that's the legacy partnership we were made for. Our work should glorify our Creator, contribute to the welfare of our neighbors, and support the kingdom of heaven we hope to someday see.

Educating yourself is a positive. There is always something you need to learn, and a focus on living the life you were created for is amazing—as long as it doesn't absorb your every waking moment, causing you to neglect important relationships. Enthusiasm on overkill will turn people off and destroy opportunities for support and partnership. But passion in moderation will not only keep you balanced but will also increase the level of energy others feel about you and what you do—and that impact may last long after you have left for your heavenly home. Fulfilling your purpose is about much more than you—and it's about much more than now.

Your Royal Call

Few understand just what an honor each breath and each day is. Jesus Christ, the Son of God and King of Kings, invites us into a personal relationship with intimate access. When we accept, we become part of his royal family, with all the privileges and purpose that come with that position.

Each morning when we awake, we are invited into a private audience with the King of Kings. Imagine him extending his glittering gold scepter, giving you exclusive entry into the holy of holies. Envision the jewels and precious metals inside his throne room as you join him for a private conversation. You have his ear; he will listen to you, and he's willing to share the wisdom of the ages—if only you will enter.

There is no greater abundance than access to the Creator of our souls. There is no deeper honor than to carry out your royal call with vigor, resolve, and gratitude. There is no more important heritage than to help further his kingdom work.

God has built unique opportunities into your everyday encounters. Start unearthing them, then grab them with fervor. Like Nancy's mother, put the same effort and energy into baking cookies as you would if you were catering the King's feast. Serving God's people is service to him. Treat every person you cross paths with as a child created in his image—because he or she is. Be willing to do the jobs no one else wants to do, with a helper's heart. A royal call is a call to sacrifice.

What occasions offer the greatest chance for you to make an enduring contribution? What have you overlooked in the past that could lead to a legacy imprint?

Begin with a spark of passion and fan it into a flame. Do more of what inspires you and less of what tires you. Focus on your strengths and accept your weaknesses, knowing that God is fired up with excitement for you.

Start your mornings with this prayer: "Heavenly Father, help me to see what you want me to see. To hear what you want me to hear. To learn what you want me to learn. To do what you want me to do. To be who you want me to be."

Ask God for the wisdom you need to discover what it is he wants from you daily so your influence can ripple into eternity. Your life is your story. Write it well. Edit often. And remember, you only get one chance to tell it.

MIND, BODY, AND SPIRIT STRENGTHENERS

YOUR ABUNDANT PURPOSE CHALLENGE

Dare to consider God's desires for you:

- Who did he create you to be?
- What did he create you to do?
- Where does he want you to be?
- When does he want you to act?
- How does he want you to live your life?
- Why would you not give yourself permission to believe in yourself as much as he believes in you?

YOUR ABUNDANT PURPOSE EXERCISE

Make a list of everything holding you back: emotions, resources, practicalities, and people. Now put them through the filter test:

- What does God say compared to what you or someone else is telling you about your ability to succeed in light of these factors?

- What would it feel like to accomplish your goals and missions, your dreams and desires?

YOUR ABUNDANT PURPOSE SCRIPTURE

Jeremiah 33:3 (NIV): "Call to me and I will answer you and tell you great and unsearchable things you do not know."

YOUR ABUNDANT PURPOSE PROMISE

You were made to experience an exceedingly passionate life with an influence that extends into eternity.

YOUR ABUNDANT PURPOSE STUDY AND DISCUSSION PROMPTS

Are you inspired and passionate about the adventure of living, or do you get bogged down by a barely-getting-by mind-set?

Are you grumbling and complaining about delays, or are you looking for the lessons, miracles, and beauty in the scenic route God is taking you on? What have you experienced that could help someone else on their quest for an abundant life?

Do you live on purpose, with purpose, in order to fulfill the exceedingly abundant purpose God designed for you? Do you recognize God's touch and your opportunity to touch others in your everyday life?

CHAPTER 15

Made for Mission

God uses the flawed and the imperfect
to accomplish His perfect will.

—Jim George, *The Basic Bible Pocket Guide*

The question Troy Gentry asked me still swirls through my mind, especially now that he's gone after a fluke helicopter accident took his life. On that hot, summer day when we met, one thought burned in his mind: "How do I find out what God's purpose is for me?"

He wanted assurance that he was doing right by God. He was a man on a quest to complete his eternal mission.

If someone with his worldly success was seeking an answer to the reason for his existence, it's no surprise that everyday people are seeking as well. Human beings are designed with a compulsion to know that what they've done is what they were supposed to have done—that they matter and have made a difference. Troy was no exception.

As part of the country music duo Montgomery Gentry, Troy was a man who loved his fans, the stage, and spreading joy. When I met him, he had his priorities in their proper place. He told me, "My wealth comes from God and family, not money or fame. I've learned the hard way, those things are full of trappings and temptation."

He was in a season of his life where he felt the most important question to ask was, "How do I find out what God's purpose is for me?"

I believe he not only found the answer, but that answer led to his making a bigger difference than he would have dreamed.

As I watched the funeral service, I was especially touched to hear "Redeemed" by Big Daddy Weave played. The song shares the message of someone set free from their past mistakes, guilt, and shame, boldly submitting to all God made them to be. Troy embraced his role as a redeemed man. He was imperfect, but he never gave up on his goal to be a better person, and his heart was obviously transformed by Christ's forever-flowing grace. Each eulogy and testimony affirmed my own encounter with Troy—but one story particularly caught my attention.

From the podium at the funeral, Troy's close friend Eddie Lunn told about a men's Bible discussion group held regularly in a Tennessee restaurant. During the last years of his life, any time he was home, Troy joined in.

Lunn said that on March 10, 2015, two and a half years after my meeting with Troy, they were talking about Jesus's response when asked which command in the law was the greatest (Matt. 22:35–40).

Troy texted his close friend after he left the breakfast meeting. "Hey, what were those two things that Jesus said if you lived by, covers all the commandments? And where may I find it?"

"Love God. Love others," Eddie Lunn texted back.

Lunn said you could feel the excitement in Troy's next texts. Like he was saying, "Wait. You mean I can do these two things and it covers everything else in the Bible? Sign me up!"

At Troy's funeral, his friend added, "This gave purpose and meaning to his desire to be a better person. This gave the *why* to being a better person. We are all wired to love God and to love others."

There is an important element I don't want us to overlook in what Eddie Lunn said. The why behind what we do is crucial to leading an exceedingly abundant life. God's overarching call for all of us is to love actively and with godly purity. This is our greatest mission. Yes, we will occasionally mess up, but with focused attention we are capable of consistency. If our aim is to love God, we need to love people. And if we do that, we can have assurance we are making right decisions for good reasons. A mission-minded focus keeps us on track, and a successful accomplishment requires preparedness.

Standing on the Ready

Most of us are ordinary people, called by a mighty God to wear our faith openly and naturally in an unassuming way. We are imperfect, flawed, and must forgive ourselves regularly; we need Jesus every single day. But we are also equipped by God through personality, background, education, and experience so we can stand on the ready for any moment he calls us to action. You must be prepared, because you never know who he will send your way.

When I met Troy Gentry, I didn't know how God would use me to affect him, nor do I take credit for anything unwarranted. The fact is, I didn't save Troy. The Father drew him, Jesus saved him, and the Holy Spirit guided him (respectively, John 6:44; 3:17; 14:26), according to God's plan. Plenty of other people were planted in Troy's life to help bring him to a committed faith walk. Some were permanent, like his wife and children, his close friends, his pastor, and his Bible study buddies. Others, like me, were sent for a moment to drop another seed.

Each of us influences someone daily. Who? Where? When? How many? Only God knows. Our job is to be ready and willing, and our assignment is obedience.

Whether it's soul talk with a close friend or a brief exchange with a celebrity, we leave an eternal imprint on people. We influence the thinking, actions, and being of strangers as well as family members. Touching lives in meaningful ways is one of the most integral pieces to fulfilling our God-designed purpose. And if we inspire and encourage, we can help others fulfill God's plans for them. How you treat people can mark them forever.

Who will God send across your path? Are you ready to answer his call to action? Don't miss your moment by constantly looking down at your phone or discounting your worth. Look up to where your purpose comes from. Look beyond your time on earth to see what lasting impression God is calling you to make.

Perfect People Need Not Apply

It's refreshing to know that for doing God's work, perfect people need not apply. We have a perfect Savior, and that's enough. God is always willing to use the willing. This is why the surprise discovery of my paternal biology and my former disobedience to God's call to pray with a stranger did not stop me from finding and fulfilling his supernatural plans. He doesn't use me because I'm worthy; he uses me because I say yes to his best—in spite of my worst.

In your everyday, in every moment, in every way, opportunity resides. Perfection is not required to make an impact. You don't have to get cleaned up to come to God. Imperfection is no excuse for inaction. Talk to him as you are, and he will take care of the cleaning. Simply trust him to do exceedingly abundantly more than you can possibly imagine. God is looking for faith, not flawlessness (Gal. 2:16).

You can be skilled, strategic, and mission-minded but still make mistakes. Just don't let them keep you from moving forward. Otherwise you may miss your chance to accomplish all you were made for. That next person you come in contact with may be the one person placed within your influence as an integral part of your daily assignment to make a difference.

Embracing the Mission

It's easy to think we have plenty of time to love people and do God's work . . . later. But if I learned anything from Troy it's that we don't always have more time to fulfill God's plan.

Watching the service online provided the comfort I'd sought after I learned of Troy's death. I believe he got the answer to his question about purpose. By the accounts shared, I believe Troy fully understood God's plans for him and passionately embraced his call to love God, love others, and serve all during his last days.

Two days before Troy died, Montgomery Gentry put the finishing touches on a new album called *Here's to You*. They always sang from their hearts, but for Troy, one song on this album was very special. When I listened to his voice belting out the lyrics of "Better Me," I smiled through sobs.

Troy sang about a man improved but still limited, a man turning his back on foolish ways, learning and fighting daily to become better. It wasn't hype. Many might not realize why this song held so much importance for Troy Gentry, but I know it was personal, very personal.

Through music, Troy publicly shared his commitment to turn away from past mistakes and his resolve to spend eternity with Jesus Christ. He just didn't know eternity was coming so soon. None of us did.

We can't know when we will take our last breath—only God does. This could be your last morning before you are in an accident, before a freak tree falls onto your house, before a disease halts your heart, before you are headed to a performance only to lose your life in a tragic crash.

All these circumstances have taken people's lives. But the point is this: though only God knows the exact moment, place, and way we will die, we can be assured we are meant to live a life of meaning to the end. Wisdom comes from that awareness. We learn appreciation and purposefulness from counting our days—not obsessively but intentionally (Ps. 90:12). This is why every second we should be prepared to meet God face-to-face. And why it's important to spend every possible breath following his will and not just our own. We must embrace the mission we are given. Consider these questions:

- If this was your last day on earth, how would God want you to spend it?
- If you knew your actions today would affect your forever as well as that of those you meet, what would you do differently?
- If you knew Jesus was coming back in the next thirty seconds—what would truly matter?

We were created to partner our efforts with God for the good of other people and his kingdom plan. Something beautiful happens for us when we do. Our own thirsty souls are satisfied.

Resolve not to let any circumstance, situation, or excuse stop you from fulfilling your high calling. Don't let age or illness keep you from living out love. Even if you have limited mobility, are a caregiver, or feel inadequate, there are things you can do to live a life of meaning every day.

Squeeze a hand. Show compassion in your conversation. Smile with your eyes. Listen with empathy. Speak encouragement. Write a note of appreciation if you're able. Pass on what you've learned. And remember that praying for others is one of the most precious and powerful ways we can change lives.

Do what you can now. Don't wait! These are the gifts you give that will echo in minds and hearts on earth after you enter eternity. When you complete God's plan, you surely make him smile.

Seeing God's Heart for Us

If you feel like your life is nothing but one big accident or mistake, think again. You exist for a reason, to execute specific plans, and I believe God desires that he would get to say those most cherished words to you: "Well done, good and faithful servant! . . . Come and share your master's happiness" (Matt. 25:21 NIV).

I also believe he wants to brag on you. What compels me to make this bold proclamation?

Because once again, we glimpse God's heart, his enthusiasm, and his passion for his people through Scripture. For example, in Exodus 31:1–5, we're told, "The LORD spoke to Moses, saying, 'See, I have called by name Bezalel, the son of Uri, the son of Hur, of the tribe of Judah. I have filled him with the Spirit of God in wisdom, in understanding, in knowledge, and in all kinds of craftsmanship, to make artistic designs for work in gold, in silver, and in bronze, and in the cutting of stones for settings, and in the carving of wood, that he may work in all kinds of craftsmanship'" (NASB).

Do you hear the delight in his voice? He is one proud Papa. Wouldn't you want to use your God-designed giftings so your Father in heaven could talk about *you* like that? Because it's no stretch to say that he wants to. What abilities has he built into you that he's waiting to watch you use?

Now let's look at Job 1:8: "The LORD said to Satan, 'Have you considered My servant Job? For there is no one like him on the earth, a blameless and upright man, fearing God and turning away from evil'" (NASB).

Can you hear God's joy spilling from his words? He is one pleased parent. What would it feel like to know God said about you, "Have you considered my servant, ___________?" How could your attitudes and actions bless your Father in heaven as he watches from above?

In these two glimpses, we see two men with two different aptitudes that God speaks highly of, and we get a taste of God's pleasure. Bezalel used his hands; Job used his heart.

Our Father has infused every man and woman with specific talents, abilities, and gifts, and he wants us to use them for good, whatever they are. But the spirit in which we go about our pursuits matters as much as what we do. God loves us unconditionally—nothing can change that—but assurance of his pleasure comes from being obedient and doing his will. For an interesting study, read through the Bible and mark every passage where you see that a person or group did what the Lord said.

Make it a practice to ask and seek what God wants you to do with your life, in your everyday and in significant ways. You can trust you will eventually find answers.

Matthew 7:7 promises that if we *seek*, we will find. There isn't a time stamp on discovery, but it's a promise you can believe. In Jeremiah 33:3, God says, "Ask me and I will tell you remarkable secrets you do not know about things to come." That's an exciting assurance.

I'm stunned at how many people make assumptions about God's plans for them, causing them to stop asking and seeking his will for their lives. I'm also dismayed at how many of us search for reasons he shouldn't use us. We can certainly find them, but by doing so, aren't we putting words in his mouth? Don't make that mistake. Instead, let him speak directly to you through the Bible, and dare to believe what you find. Listen to his whispers in your spirit. And go throughout your days seeking your purpose until you unearth it.

Live Like You Believe Him

In Jesus's parable of the talents, each person was given a number of talents based on his abilities, much like the abilities given to Bezalel, Job, and us. When I researched the root word for "abilities" used in the parable, I discovered it comes from the Greek word *dunamai*.

Dunamai is defined as "to be able, to have power."[1] If you want to experience the exceedingly abundant life Christ promised, and to fulfill every mission you are called to, then live like you believe in the abilities you've been given. The great I Am makes you able. The great I Am makes you powerful. You have the ability to do the seemingly impossible.

I've heard people say, "The purpose of life is to end." That kind of thinking won't lead to hope or a sense of usefulness. But it might lead to despair. I disagree with this pessimistic view. I believe the purpose of life is to relish every day rooted in a fresh-start mind-set, acting with fresh faith and resolved to live with fresh purpose. We can make a difference where we are while we live.

At the end of your life, neither your possessions, your position, or your profession will hold your hand or welcome you to your true home in heaven. You can't take what you've accumulated on earth into eternity, so don't allow things to take priority over people. Be the best friend, spouse, parent, sibling, child, coworker, servant, and stranger you can be while you are here.

Invest time and energy into developing and maintaining loving relationships that will sustain you in your final days. Invest yourself in the healthy pursuit of the dreams, passions, and desires God wired into you. Look for a higher call, no matter what you face or who you meet. And pass on your purpose so it thrives after you are gone.

One day, if we follow God's approach, we will pass from this life to an even more beautiful life. But until then, we have many reasons to continue living with purpose because we are highly valued by our Maker. His plans always leave a positive mark.

"Love the Lord your God with all your heart, soul, mind, and strength. And love your neighbor as yourself." This summary clearly defines your high calling and priority assignment in Jesus's own words.

Dare to be you and to make the difference only you can make.

If there's one lesson Troy Gentry taught me it's that real living means grabbing each day intentionally. We were not made for a wimpy existence. Our God made us to be brave and bold and to live with exclamation! Those who succeed are willing to act courageously and consistently when others are not.

I hope this book has helped you discover a reason to get out of bed in the morning and has provided revelations about the real reasons you exist. May the stories you've read and the skills and strategies we've discussed inspire you to go on an intentional odyssey to find out why you were made. I hope you see that when you seek God, your life on earth will touch others in meaningful ways and your purpose will reverberate beyond your final breath.

Whenever and wherever you live out God's love, you will have unearthed and achieved something amazing. More than anything, people on this planet are hungry for godly acceptance, even when they don't realize it, and you can change their lives by offering them this priceless treasure. Pour into others, and blessings of various kinds will pour into you.

No matter how life started for you, do not question this truth: you exist on purpose, with purpose, and you are meant to fulfill an extraordinary purpose. You are meant to experience exceedingly abundantly more than you can possibly imagine. You were also made for your Maker's pleasure and passion. You are his child, and your inheritance is secure.

Some day, maybe sooner than you think, you will stand before the

One who crafted you in your mother's womb. Close your eyes and imagine hearing him say, "Well done, my good and faithful servant. (Insert your name) _______________, come share your master's happiness." In whatever way the details of your purpose takes shape, be assured this is the mission and ultimate "more" you were made for. The question is, Will you dare believe?

MIND, BODY, AND SPIRIT STRENGTHENERS

YOUR ABUNDANT PURPOSE CHALLENGE

Determine not to hide your faith. You don't have to be loud and proud, attempting to shove God down people's throats. Neither should you hide the light of Christ's goodness in your life. You never know who you might illuminate.

YOUR ABUNDANT PURPOSE EXERCISE

Make God's love law your mantra—the filter you pour everything through. Start your day with this reminder: love the Lord your God, love people, and love yourself. Write it down and place it where you will run across it, and mentally call on this vital cleanser when you need assurance for what to do.

YOUR ABUNDANT PURPOSE SCRIPTURE

Isaiah 46:10 (NIV): "I make known the end from the beginning, from ancient times, what is still to come. I say, 'My purpose will stand, and I will do all that I please.'"

YOUR ABUNDANT PURPOSE PROMISE

God's purpose always leaves a mark. So be assured, you are made to make an eternal impression. This is your ultimate call.

YOUR ABUNDANT PURPOSE STUDY AND DISCUSSION PROMPTS

Who has made the most significant impact on you? Which of that person's traits would you like to emulate in your own life?

EXCEEDINGLY

Do you dare to ask and praise God in advance for providing exceedingly abundantly more than you can think or imagine?

When you leave your body, what is it about your spirit that people will most remember? In what ways will you leave the world better than when you were born? What will the most meaningful imprint you leave look like?

ACKNOWLEDGMENTS

There are more people than I could possibly name who have made this book possible, but some played such an obvious role that they require public appreciation.

Thank you, Ricky. You, dear husband, more than anyone, see the sacrifice, the hours, and the struggles required for me to live the life of a writer. You provide wisdom when I'm torn in different directions. You encourage me when I'm down. You make me laugh when I feel like crying. Your kindness and support mean so much. As I often say, I don't just love you, I adore you.

I am grateful to my sons, Madison and Ryan. Each of you in your own unique way provides me with strength and energy. Just looking at your faces makes me know I am fulfilling my purpose. I'm very thankful each of you was born.

To my four beautiful grandchildren: God wired each of you especially special, and I am glad you were sent to our family. Thank you for giving me an excuse to get down and play, and for giving your PaPa Ricky and me much to look forward to.

Beth Brooks, you are the daughter I never birthed but am so happy to have. Through your quiet grace, inner beauty, forgiving attitude, and lovely smile, God gave you a distinctive purpose. I sometimes watch you in amazement and awe, just so delighted that my grandchildren get to be raised by you.

I am thankful for my advance readers and editors: Suzanne Kuhn, Jessica Bostick, Ashley Caudle, Lisa Eckman, Laura Tarvin, Dee Dee Everett, Sharon England, and Jena Gillam. Your enthusiasm and expertise made this book so much better, and I cannot adequately express my gratitude. Darla, Cindy, and Wanda, I am indebted for your early encouragement.

Janyre, your word scalpel provided the precision this manuscript desperately needed. You deserve an extra vacation after the work you've done to make this book better.

Karen Jordan and Kathryn Graves, you impact everything I write in positive ways. Thank you for the pushes as well as the pulls, for the prayers as well as the edit suggestions, and for the triple-cord friendship I can always count on. I would not be where I am today if God hadn't used you both to teach and inspire me.

My Diva Prayer Sisters, I deeply appreciate our group. Thank you for providing a place to bring prayer requests and praise reports. I love each of you uniquely.

Mary Ransom, Karen Jones, and Chris Krone, you are my safe place to land. I am grateful for our moments of laughter as well as your shoulders to cry on. When I need a break from the writing, our girls' days out refuel and energize me. Thanks for playing and praying with me.

To my CLC Rolla church family, I love doing life with all of you. Thank you for your acceptance, encouragement, and support. I'm so glad perfect people aren't allowed to attend, otherwise I'd be out. Most of all, I appreciate a worship environment with strong biblical teaching, based on living out Jesus's example to love unconditionally. Pastors Eddie and Karen, and Chris and Stacy, you fan my passion to honor God in all I do.

To my siblings, we share history no one else can understand. You helped shape me, and I am glad God chose you. I am privileged to be your sister.

Mom, I do not know how to express the depth of my gratitude for all you have done—not just for me, but for all your children and grandchildren. You are a difference maker who doesn't realize her own impact. I can't imagine anyone else being my mother, and for that I am blessed.

To my birth father, wherever you are, and my dad who raised me, thank you for helping make me who I am. Each of your contributions gave me life. I appreciate it.

And finally, to the team at Kregel Publications, thank you for believing in this book from concept to manuscript. May our partnership make a difference in the lives of many.

NOTES

CHAPTER 3: MADE FOR PRESENCE

1. Steve Bradt, "Wandering Mind Not a Happy Mind," *Harvard Gazette*, November 11, 2010, https://news.harvard.edu/gazette/story/2010/11/wandering-mind-not-a-happy-mind/.

CHAPTER 4: MADE FOR COURAGE

1. *Merriam-Webster*, s.v. "take (*v.*)," accessed December 26, 2018, https://www.merriam-webster.com/dictionary/take.
2. *Merriam-Webster*, s.v. "courage (*n.*)," accessed December 26, 2018, https://www.merriam-webster.com/dictionary/courage.

CHAPTER 5: MADE FOR PLAY

1. *Merriam-Webster*, s.v. "play (*n.*)," accessed December 26, 2018, https://www.merriam-webster.com/dictionary/play.

CHAPTER 6: MADE FOR RELATIONSHIP

1. Liz Mineo, "Good Genes Are Nice, but Joy Is Better," *Harvard Gazette*, April 11, 2017, https://news.harvard.edu/gazette/story/2017/04/over-nearly-80-years-harvard-study-has-been-showing-how-to-live-a-healthy-and-happy-life.
2. Robert Waldinger, "What Makes a Good Life? Lessons from the Longest Study on Happiness," TEDxBeaconStreet, November 2015, TED video, 12:47, https://www.ted.com/talks/robert_waldinger_what_makes_a_good_life_lessons_from_the_longest_study_on_happiness.

NOTES

CHAPTER 9: MADE FOR LEADERSHIP

1. Zig Ziglar, *Secrets of Closing the Sale: For Anyone Who Must Get Others to Say Yes!* (Grand Rapids: Revell, 1984), 22.

CHAPTER 12: MADE FOR FRUITFULNESS

1. *Merriam-Webster*, s.v. "abundance (*n.*)," accessed December 26, 2018, https://www.merriam-webster.com/dictionary/abundance.
2. *Merriam-Webster*, s.v. "prosperity (*n.*)," accessed December 26, 2018, https://www.merriam-webster.com/dictionary/prosperity.
3. *Strong's Concordance*, s.v. "perissos," BibleHub, accessed December 26, 2018, https://biblehub.com/greek/4053.htm.
4. *Strong's Concordance*, s.v. "huperekperissou," BibleHub, accessed December 26, 2018, https://biblehub.com/greek/5238b.htm.

CHAPTER 13: MADE FOR POWER

1. *Strong's Concordance*, s.v. "Chananyah," BibleHub, accessed December 26, 2018, https://biblehub.com/hebrew/2608.htm.
2. *Strong's Concordance*, s.v. "Mishael," BibleHub, accessed December 26, 2018, https://biblehub.com/hebrew/4333.htm.
3. *Strong's Concordance*, s.v. "Azaryah or Azaryahu," BibleHub, accessed December 26, 2018, https://biblehub.com/hebrew/5838.htm.
4. See "YHVH" and "El" on "Hebrew Names and Titles of God," Hebrew for Christians, accessed December 26, 2018, https://hebrew4christians.com/Names_of_G-d/names_of_g-d.html.
5. *Merriam-Webster*, s.v. "gracious (*adj.*)," accessed December 26, 2018, https://www.merriam-webster.com/dictionary/gracious.

CHAPTER 15: MADE FOR MISSION

1. *Strong's Concordance*, s.v. "dunamai," BibleHub, accessed December 26, 2018, https://biblehub.com/str/greek/1410.htm.